As NIGHT Comes On

As NIGHT Comes On

Strengthening the Things That Remain

WARREN B. SMITH

MOUNTAIN STREAM PRESS

As Night Comes On: Strengthening the Things That Remain

Mountain Stream Press
To order additional copies of this book call 866-876-3910 (U.S./CA). For international orders, call 541-391-7699 or visit www.newage-toamazinggrace.com, the author's website.

Publisher's Cataloging-in-Publication Data

Smith, Warren B.
As night comes on / Warren B. Smith.
224 pages cm
Includes endnotes.

ISBN 978-0-9846461-8-0 (softbound : alk. paper) 1. Christianity 2. Encouragement 3. Bible verses 4. Discernment 5. New age movement

---

Printed in the United States of America

CONTENTS

I must work the works of him that sent
me, while it is day: the night cometh,
when no man can work. (John 9:4)

PROLOGUE

In my ninth-grade Latin class, we always corrected each other's tests. Each student would then publicly announce his score to the teacher and the class. One unforgettable day, we graded and reported our test scores as usual. When it came around to me, I reluctantly disclosed my score—"40!" Looking at me intently and not mincing his words, the teacher ominously stated—"Mr. Smith, evil days are upon you!"

Already feeling bad enough about having to openly share my awful score, I was thrown into further dismay by my teacher's stern reprimand. How could he say something like that to me in front of the whole class? However, many years later, as I found myself speaking at prophecy conferences, I realized I was telling everyone the very same thing, yet in a completely different and biblical context—"evil days are upon you!"

Over the last fifty years, concerned individuals and various discernment ministries have tried to warn the church about the New Age/New Spirituality and its increasing influence on the lives of countless believers. However, it seems that most church leaders have consistently ignored these warnings. As a result, our Spiritual Adversary has made huge inroads into today's church as he paves the way for his New World Religion and his false Christ—the Antichrist. Attempting to deconstruct biblical Christianity, he is simultaneously constructing his New

Gospel/New Spirituality while today's church is walking right into his spiritual trap.

As night comes on, and while the world and the church continue their free fall into spiritual deception, an obvious question arises: *How does one stand in the face of what is happening?*

Hopefully, what is presented in this book will help to strengthen all of us as we hold fast to God's Word and the true Christ—Jesus Christ. May the Lord bless you, keep you, and encourage you *because*—evil days are definitely upon us.

> Be watchful, and strengthen the things
> which remain. (Revelation 2:25)

1

The Big Picture

Lest Satan should get an advantage of us: for we are not ignorant of his devices. (2 Corinthians 2:11)

In a front page article in the September 27, 2007, *Fresno Bee* newspaper, the headline read: "Going in the Wrong direction." The article was about hikers who end up getting lost—even dying—as a result of their stepping off of an established trail in Yosemite National Park. The sub-heading read, "It just takes one misstep for even the most experienced hikers to go missing." The article begins:

> It's called the "cascade effect"—a catchy name for the way one mistake leads to another, and a quick explanation for how a hiker who takes one step off of an established trail is one step closer to trouble.

The account goes on:

> Park rangers and search and rescue experts say that hundreds of hikers take that one wrong step each year. The key, they say, is where that next step takes them—back toward the trail or further down a perilous path.

The Bible also talks of a perilous path—one that has "a form of godliness" (2 Timothy 3:5) but is not from God. For those who have a love of the truth and endeavor to keep God's Word, it is of utmost importance to not be deceived into stepping off the narrow path onto a perilous path that leads to death and destruction (Matthew 7:13-14).

SATAN'S TEMPTING DEVICES

SCRIPTURE MAKES IT clear that we have a Spiritual Adversary, Satan the Devil, who is constantly tempting us with his cunning devices. We are warned that he comes as "an angel of light" and his ministers as "ministers of righteousness" (2 Corinthians 11:14-15). Because his deceptive devices can be very appealing, the apostle Paul tells us—"Study to shew thyself approved unto God, a workman that needeth not to be ashamed, rightly dividing the word of truth" (2 Timothy 2:15).

Paul stressed the importance of not being ignorant of Satan's devices lest he get an advantage of us (2 Corinthians 2:11). He said "it is a shame even to speak of those things which are done of them in secret" but they must be "reproved" and brought to the "light" (Ephesians 5:12-13).

GOD'S PLAN VS. THE DEVIL'S PLAN

GOD HAS A plan, the plan of salvation, but the Devil has a plan too—a plan of destruction. So, again, we are not to be ignorant of this deceptive plan and its accompanying devices. We must try to understand the "big picture" so to speak. Why? In case we suddenly find ourselves on the "broad way" path to Antichrist rather than the "narrow way" path to Jesus Christ.

Jesus warned that prior to His return "false Christs" and "false prophets" would arise and show "great signs and wonders"

(Matthew 24:24). In that same verse, He said the deception would be so great that—"if it were possible"—even the "elect" would be deceived. So what is the "big picture?" What is Satan's plan?

SATAN'S NEW AGE PEACE PLAN

ALL OF SATAN'S devices are designed to accomplish one major objective—to get his man, the Antichrist, into position. The prophet Daniel warned that the Antichrist will have a deceptive peace plan and "by peace shall destroy many" (Daniel 8:25). He further warned that this deceptive peace plan would "destroy wonderfully" because it will appear to be so *wonderful* (Daniel 8:24).

Who doesn't want world peace? But peace from what source and on what terms? Presently, this deceptive peace plan is floating under the radar as "God's Dream" for the world, the church, and the coming "New Age." But first, what exactly *is* New Age?

WHAT IS THE NEW AGE?

I WAS FIRST introduced to the concept of "God's Dream" and the "God's Dream" peace plan after being seduced into what has been popularly referred to as the New Age movement. In its simplest terms, the New Age movement was, and still is, a deceptive spiritual movement that goes all the way back to the Garden of Eden. It was there, at the beginning of creation, that the serpent cast doubt on God's Word while simultaneously suggesting that men could be like God (Genesis 3:1-5).

Emerging from its semi-veiled occult obscurity, the New Age movement suddenly burst forth amidst a growing drug culture and the social and political unrest of the 1960s and 1970s. It seemed to offer an exciting and adventurous spiritual alternative to what was perceived by many to be a tired, outdated, and obsolete Christian faith.

Gathering momentum in the 1980s and beyond, what was formerly called the occult, and then the New Age, is now mainstream. In the late 1990s and into the new millennium, the term New Age *seemed* to disappear. But the New Age never went away as most people thought—it was simply repackaged as a New Gospel, a New Spirituality, and a New Worldview. Over the past two decades, this New Age/New Spirituality/New Worldview has not only integrated itself into the world, but has made great inroads into the church itself. However, as a rose by any other name is still a rose, so the New Age by any other name is still the New Age.

In a nutshell, the New Age/New Spirituality is based on the foundational false teaching that all of humanity is "One" because God is alleged to be "in" everyone and everything. And because God is said to be "in" everyone and everything, we are all "connected" because "we are all God." This foundational bottom line of the New Age belief system was captured in a photograph sent to me by a pastor in southern California. In the photo, a young man is wearing a T-shirt that says—"I used to be an atheist until I realized I was God."

However, man is *not* God, and God is *not* "in" everyone and everything (Psalm 39:5). God makes it clear in Hosea 11:9 when He says, "for I am God, and not man." Galatians 6:3 states, "For if a man think himself to be something, when he is nothing, he deceiveth himself." Ezekiel 28:2 says—"yet thou art a man, and not God, though thou set thine heart as the heart of God." Nevertheless, all of Satan's devices are cunningly devised to bring the world—and the church—to believe this foundational lie that God is "in" everyone and everything. But, "If the foundations be destroyed, what can the righteous do?" (Psalm 11:3).

Many years ago, I was recruited into the New Age to help implement its deceptive peace plan. Many of the devices used to deceive me into accepting its teachings are the same devices being used today to deceive the world—and the church. These devices are preparing everyone for a seemingly "wonderful" peace plan that is being euphemistically described as "God's Dream for the world." The following are ten of these deceptive spiritual devices.

Ten Spiritual Devices

1) Putting Unwarranted Trust in People

My involvement in the New Age was not initiated by an interest in spirituality, but by my interest in a waitress at a local downtown restaurant. One day, she mentioned that a friend of a friend of hers was a psychic and was coming to town to do some psychic readings. She asked if I would be interested in seeing this woman and getting a reading. Wanting to demonstrate my being open to spiritual things, and hoping to gain her favor, I agreed to see the psychic.

Had it not been for my friend's endorsement of this questionable practice, I would never have consented to the reading. However, my natural suspicion of psychics was overridden by her making it seem so normal. Later as a new Christian, I read in the Bible how spiritually dangerous it is to be involved with psychics. We are not to give *any* regard to those who consult with familiar spirits (Leviticus 19:31). Psychics, and things like Ouija Boards, Tarot Cards, meditation, Yoga, interacting with the dead, and countless other occult practices can unwittingly open doors to a deceptive and very evil spirit world.

Sadly, this same device of putting unwarranted trust in people, rather than the Word of God, can also be seen in the church today. Just because a friend, relative, or church leader has been a Christian for years, doesn't mean that their endorsement of a particular pastor, teacher, book, or spiritual practice should be accepted without any questions.

The Bible warns us not to put undue trust in a friend or a guide. Rather, we are to "try the spirits" (1 John 4:1) and rightly divide the Word of God regarding whatever we are reading, experiencing, or being told (2 Timothy 2:15). Like the Bereans, we are to search the Scriptures daily to see if these things are really "so" (Acts 17:11). Trusting other people and not the Word of God is one of Satan's many deceptive devices.

> Trust ye not in a friend, put ye not confidence in a guide. (Micah 7:5)

2) Putting Unwarranted Trust in Spiritual Experiences

During my spiritual reading with the psychic, she revealed many things about me that she had no way of knowing. This made her more credible in my eyes and she gained my immediate respect and definite attention. Toward the end of the reading, I felt an intense whirling sensation over my head that vibrated and tingled and felt very strange. I had never experienced anything quite like it.

Without my saying anything to her, the psychic said—"Are you aware there is a ball of light over your head right now?" She proceeded to tell me that the ball of light was there because I had "a lot of help on the other side." When I asked her what the "other side" was, she told me the spirit world—loved ones who had passed on, angels, and other spirits who were interested in my spiritual well-being. She said if I wanted their help in my spiritual life, I simply had to ask and give them permission to come into my life.

So that night I prayed—"All you on the other side, I want your help in my life, I want to become more spiritual, I want to grow." In my naiveté, what I actually prayed was a reverse sinner's prayer that was completely contrary to God's ways. By doing this, I had unwittingly opened a door to the evil spirit world.

When I came to the Lord and gained a better understanding of the Bible, I realized the ball of light that appeared in my psychic reading was not good and was not from God. It was obviously a deceptive spirit that came as an angel of light. It was sent to make me feel special and to convince me that I had a lot of spiritual help on "the other side." And the psychic told me that part of that help might come from "loved ones" who had passed on. This alleged communication with the dead was very common in the New Age, but it is not usually found in the church.

However, a prominent pastor in Tennessee, claims that he and his wife have had "meetings"[1] with their deceased son. In their book *Have Heart: Bridging the Gulf Between Heaven and Earth*, Steve and Sarah Berger describe some of their son's alleged appearances. Endorsements by mega-church pastor Greg Laurie, televangelist James Robison, and others listed in the front of their book, seem to give legitimacy to what they are teaching—just as the waitress seemed to give legitimacy to my seeing a psychic. But, again, we are not to put unquestioned trust in people rather than the Word of God.

The Bible is very clear that we are not to communicate with the dead. This is the stuff of séances, channelings, spiritist readings, and the occult/New Age. Deuteronomy 18:9-11 forbids interacting with the dead and calls it necromancy. Certain pastors may have fairly solid reputations as teachers and evangelists, but they are seriously wrong to present this kind of teaching to the church. The evil spirit world is only too willing to counterfeit our loved ones through spiritual experiences that play upon our human emotions and our love of family. Providing deceptive spiritual experiences that can open doors to the spirit world is one of Satan's chief devices.

> Now the Spirit speaketh expressly, that in the latter times some shall depart from the faith, giving heed to seducing spirits, and doctrines of devils. (1 Timothy 4:1)

3) Seemingly "Meant–To–Be" Circumstances That Appear to Be From God

Later the same year that I had seen the psychic, I took a trip to Big Sur for a special New Year's Eve. This rugged California coastal area seemed to be a great place to continue my spiritual pursuits and start the year. Walking into the majestic Nepenthe bookstore, I was immediately drawn to a book titled *Journey Toward the Heart* by an Indian master I had never heard of before—Bhagwan Shree Rajneesh.

After a series of *seemingly* "meant-to-be" circumstances that arose immediately after purchasing the book by Rajneesh, I serendipitously landed in a mountaintop cabin with nothing but clouds below us and, incredibly, another book by Rajneesh—*Only One Sky*—sitting on the bedside table. Bhagwan Shree Rajneesh—a man I had never heard of before purchasing his other book an hour previous. Everything seemed to be benevolently conspiring to introduce me to this Indian guru. It all seemed so "meant-to-be." But the question I never thought to ask was, meant-to-be by *whom*?

Many pastors, church leaders, and plain everyday folks are fond of saying: "It's no accident." "There is a reason for everything." "It was meant-to-be." The inference is that whatever they experienced was good and must have been divinely orchestrated by God. Rarely, if ever, does anyone even hint at the possibility of spiritual deception. But many of today's spiritual experiences are *not* from God. It may seem to be God or Jesus or the Holy Spirit when it is not.

Thus, whatever one is experiencing or being told needs to be tested, prayed about, and rightly divided by the Word of God. And while God can also orchestrate spiritual experiences, the church should always be on the lookout for contrived meant-to-be circumstances arranged by our Spiritual Adversary. These deceptive, seemingly meant-to-be experiences are yet another one of Satan's clever devices.

> These things have I written unto you concerning them that seduce you. (1 John 2:26)

4) The New Age Doctrine of "Oneness"

In 1980, New Age author Marilyn Ferguson's book *The Aquarian Conspiracy* was published and became an instant cult classic. In this book that is often regarded as a New Age Bible, Ferguson wrote, with tongue-in-cheek, that a growing number of New Age "conspirators" had "a great heretical idea"—the notion of "God within"—that God was "in" everyone and everything.[2] As I fell deeper and deeper under the spiritual spell of Rajneesh and my other New Age teachers, this God "in" everyone and everything concept of Oneness seemed so simple and true, and felt so right to my misguided heart.

In a booklet titled *Be Still and Know That You Are Not God: God is Not "in" Everyone and Everything,*[3] I documented how this New Age teaching of God "in" everyone and everything is not only in the world but also in the church. It isn't just New Age leaders who are proclaiming it. I described how church leaders like Rick Warren, the late Eugene Peterson, Leonard Sweet, the late Sarah Young, Pope Francis, and William P. Young, among others, have brought this God "in" everything teaching into the church itself.

The Bible states that all of humanity is one blood (Acts 17:26) because we all have an original set of parents—Adam and Eve. But Jesus said what "is born of the flesh is flesh" and what "is born of the Spirit is spirit" (John 3:6). That is why He then said to "Marvel not" that we "must be born again" (John 3:7). Scripture makes it clear that God and Christ are not inherently "in" everyone and everything. It is only when we believe in Jesus Christ as our Lord and Savior and are born again that God's Holy Spirit is sent to dwell within us (John 14:26) and that we become one in Him. Christ is not in everyone, but we are one in Christ when we believe in Him and are born again—"for ye are all one in Christ Jesus" (Galatians 3:28).

The New Age "Doctrine of Oneness" that says God is "in" everyone and everything is *a lie*. It is, perhaps, Satan's chief device to deceive the world and the church. As seen with His response to the Tower of Babel, God demonstrated that He is definitely not into worldly oneness:

> And the LORD said, Behold, the people is one, and they have all one language; and this they begin to do: and now nothing will be restrained from them, which they have imagined to do. Go to, let us go down, and there confound their language, that they may not understand one another's speech. So the LORD scattered them abroad from thence upon the face of all the earth: and they left off to build the city. (Genesis 11:6-8)

5) The New Age Doctrine of Separation

While attending a massage program at the Sacramento Holistic Health Institute, one of my New Age classmates gave me a book titled *Love is Letting Go of Fear* by a psychiatrist named Gerald Jampolsky. This little self-help manual was very engaging as he talked of love, hope, faith, gratitude, and forgiveness in a decidedly unique and spiritual way. The author said his book had been greatly inspired by a set of books called *A Course in Miracles.*

I immediately purchased the *Course* at a local New Age bookstore. I was surprised to see that the books were said to be channeled from "Jesus" to a Columbia Presbyterian Hospital psychologist in New York City named Helen Schucman. Not knowing the Bible, I read and accepted what this alleged "Jesus" said and taught. I had no idea that mingled with lofty statements about God and love and the Holy Spirit, this false Christ "Jesus" turned the actual teachings of the Bible upside down and inside out.

Emphasizing the word "separation," he taught, "The recognition of God is the recognition of yourself. There is no separation of God and His creation."[4] Also emphasizing the word "oneness," he stated that "The oneness of the Creator and the creation is your wholeness, your sanity and your limitless power."[5] This counterfeit "Jesus" disparages the true Christ's victory on the Cross of Calvary by teaching that "The journey to the cross should be the last 'useless journey'"[6] and that "a slain Christ has no meaning."[7]

These teachings reiterated what I had already been learning from Rajneesh and my other New Age teachers—that we don't need an external Savior because we can save ourselves by recognizing that "we are all one" because God is "in" everyone and everything.

In her book *The Revelation*, the late New Age author, channeler, and futurist Barbara Marx Hubbard quotes the New Age Christ stating that those who oppose the idea of oneness with God are under the "illusion of separation."[8] In *A Course in Miracles*, the false New Age Christ states, "The mind can make the belief in separation very real and very fearful, and this belief is the 'devil.'"[9] He further states that those who are under the illusion of separation are dreaming and need to be "gently awakened" from their hapless dream of "separateness" by God's "happy dream" of Oneness.[10]

There is something that should be of great concern to those keeping an eye on how this concept of separation is filtering into the church: On the fifth episode of his TBN television series *Restoring the Shack*, William P. Young, citing God as his source, stated that the "lie of separation" has prevented the church from being unified, whole, and one.[11] That Young would introduce the New Age Doctrine of Separation is not surprising if you read *The Shack* carefully. *The Shack*'s "Jesus" openly teaches New Age "Oneness" when Young has him affirm that God is "in" everyone and everything. *The Shack*'s "Jesus" states, "God who is the ground of all being, dwells in, around, and through all things."[12] In *Jesus Calling*, Sarah Young's "Jesus" also teaches this same New Age Oneness when he declares—"I am above all, as well as in all."[13]

A more detailed description of this Oneness vs. Separation heresy is carefully documented in my book *False Christ Coming: Does Anybody Care*? and in a booklet titled *Oneness vs. Separation Heresy Now in the Church*. The New Age Doctrine of Separation denigrates those who refuse to subscribe to the Doctrine of Oneness. However, God *is* separate from His creation. He is not *in* everyone and everything. But Satan's twisted New Age take on separation has been—and will continue to be—one of his main devices. Using the word separation scripturally and properly, the Bible tells us to "be ye separate" from the world and from worldly New Age doctrines like the Doctrines of Oneness and Separation.

> Wherefore come out from among them, and be ye separate. (2 Corinthians 6:17)

6) God's Dream

The term "God's Dream" has become almost commonplace in the world—and the church. "God's Dream" is now the subject of numerous Christian books, booklets, sermons, songs, and radio shows. But most people using the term "God's Dream" don't realize it is a deceptive New Age term that was introduced over a hundred years ago in a 1916 *Theosophical Path* New Age magazine article.[14]

As previously mentioned, the term "God's Dream" is a crucial New Age concept intimately linked to the New Age peace plan. It is at the heart of everything taught in *A Course in Miracles* by the New Age "Jesus." The term "God's Dream" has also been used by the false Christ Maitreya who claims to already be here on Earth waiting for humanity to call him forth. It has been used by New Age channeler and best-selling *Conversations with God* author Neale Donald Walsch who claims to speak for God. It has been used and publicly promoted by New Age sympathizer Oprah Winfrey. All these references and many others are documented in my books *Evangullible* and *The Titanic and Today's Church,* and a booklet titled *God's Dream: Satan's Ultimate Scheme.*[15]

The New Age term, "God's Dream," is also used by a wide variety of pastors, Christian authors, church leaders, and worship leaders. "God's Dream" was first introduced into the church by the late Crystal Cathedral pastor Robert Schuller in his 1974 book *Your Church Has Real Possibilities.*[16] It was then exponentially popularized by Saddleback Church pastor Rick Warren. It is now commonly used by a wide array of church figures that include Bethel Church pastor Bill Johnson, Kenneth Copeland, Brian McLaren, Pope Francis, Joel Osteen, William Paul Young, Sarah Young, Leonard Sweet, Mark Batterson, Joyce Meyer, Richard Rohr, and countless others. Most of them probably have no idea of its New Age origin and how "God's Dream" is a strategic part of Satan's New Age peace plan.

Curiously, Rick Warren introduced his own formal P.E.A.C.E. Plan that he actually titled—"God's Dream for You and the World." Over the years he has pushed "God's Dream" heavily in sermons and radio programs—even writing a booklet titled *God's Dream For Your Life*. But "God's Dream" is a false overlapping New Age concept that has now made its way deep into the church. Thanks to Robert Schuller and Rick Warren, the concept of "God's Dream" has become so widely popularized in church circles that church references now outweigh the New Age references that once preceded them. "God's Dream" is one of Satan's most cunning devices.

> Behold, I am against them that prophesy false dreams, saith the LORD, and do tell them, and cause my people to err by their lies, and by their lightness; yet I sent them not, nor commanded them: therefore they shall not profit this people at all, saith the LORD. (Jeremiah 23:32)

7) Not Testing the Spirits

With Rajneesh, the psychics and channelers I spent time with, the workshops I went to, and all the New Age books I read—meditation and contemplative prayer were almost always stressed. Being still was supposed to help us attain personal peace and well-being and to hear from God—or what was often called the "Universe" or the "Source." It was through these meditative and contemplative practices that so many heretical teachings have been delivered into the world by seducing spirits—much of it described as "new revelation."

Today, there is increased pressure for people in the church to "hear the voice of God." And while countless books have been written on how to hear the voice of God, it is hard to find even one that talks about proving the authenticity of who and what they are hearing (1 Thessalonians 5:21)—to "test" and "try" the spirits because there are so many false prophets and deceptive spirits out there in the world (1 John 4:1-3, 1 Timothy 4:1).

The late Sarah Young claimed to be getting messages from Jesus, but many of her messages in *Jesus Calling* have serious New Age implications—like her "Jesus" stating that he is "in" everything—that he is "above all as well as in all."[17] *Shack* author William P. Young claims to have had conversations with God yet has his "Jesus" teaching the New Age Doctrine of Oneness—God dwelling "in" everyone and everything.[18]

We can test or try the spirits by measuring or comparing what is being said with the Word of God. If a supposed message (or messenger) from God contradicts God's Word and the Gospel message, then we know that spirit is not of God. In the case of the "Jesus" in *Jesus Calling* and *The Shack*, where he teaches that God is "in" everything and everyone, this clearly is the teaching of "another spirit" (2 Corinthians 11:4).

It is yet another one of Satan's most cunning devices to get Christian leaders and everyday believers to overlook, forget, omit, ignore, or somehow disbelieve in the necessity of testing the spirits.

> Beloved, believe not every spirit, but try the spirits whether they are of God: because many false prophets are gone out into the world. Hereby know ye the Spirit of God: Every spirit that confesseth that Jesus Christ is come in the flesh is of God: And every spirit that confesseth not that Jesus Christ is come in the flesh is not of God: and this is that spirit of antichrist, whereof ye have heard that it should come; and even now already is it in the world. (1 John 4:1-3)

8) The New Narrative/New Story

New Age leaders are teaching that we need a "new narrative"—a "new story" to replace what is perceived to be the tired "old story" of biblical Christianity. As mentioned, the "Jesus" of *A Course in Miracles* teaches the alleged "new story" of the necessity of humanity being "awakened" from its "fearful" ungodly dream of "separation" by "God's Dream" of "Oneness."

The "new story"—"God's Dream"—teaches that as humanity awakens to the truth of Oneness, world peace becomes a real possibility. But the new story warns that those who are under the "illusion of separation"—those who do not believe that God is "in" everyone and everything—hinder and prevent world peace through their disbelief.

Thus, the new story of "God's Dream" for the world and the church isolates those who do not hold to the New Age Doctrine of Oneness—like biblical Christians—and will ultimately lead to persecution. Biblical believers are disparagingly referred to as those who believe the "old story" of separation. But the Bible's story is not old in that pejorative sense. It is as true today as when it was originally written and recorded. Humanity is *not* God, and humanity is *not* one with God. God and His creation are separate. "God's Dream" is not a new story. Rather it is a cunningly devised fable that is just another one of Satan's clever devices.

> For we have not followed cunningly devised fables, when we made known unto you the power and coming of our Lord Jesus Christ, but were eyewitnesses of his majesty. (2 Peter 1:16)

9) Quantum Spirituality

When I was involved with New Age spirituality, Fritjof Capra's 1975 book *The Tao of Physics: An Exploration of the Parallels*

Between Modern Physics and Eastern Mysticism was a New Age classic. Capra contended that quantum physics was in the process of proving that God was a force and an energy field that interpenetrated all creation.

And with quantum physics leading the way, a New Age/ New Spirituality was gearing up to make both a proverbial and literal "quantum leap" to a "quantum spirituality" and a "quantum Christ"—not the biblical Christ but a New Age "God" and "Christ" who were "in" everyone and everything. Back then, I didn't know that the Bible warned about those who falsely use science to try and prove their faith (1 Timothy 6:20-21).

Sadly, church figures like Leonard Sweet are joining this march to New Age Oneness by way of quantum physics. In his 1991 book *Quantum Spirituality*, Sweet openly proclaims his belief in Oneness by quoting Catholic mystic Thomas Merton:

> We are already one. But we imagine we are not. And what we have to recover is our original unity.[19]

Sweet's New Age sympathies become even more apparent when he states that this Oneness and original unity is based on his assumed belief that God is "in" everyone and everything. He writes that his view of postmodern Christianity—spell that New Age Christianity—"entails a radical doctrine of embodiment of God in the very substance of creation."[20] My former New Age teachers couldn't have said it any more clearly than what Sweet is telling the church.

An ordained Methodist pastor who speaks all over the world, Sweet has led workshops with Rick Warren—and is, indeed, teaching the church a "radical doctrine"—the New Age Doctrine of Oneness. Compounding his New Age sympathies, Sweet refers to the father of the New Age movement—Catholic Jesuit priest Pierre Teilhard de Chardin—as "Twentieth-century Christianity's major voice."[21]

Sweet also talks openly about the importance of "God's Dream."[22] While Sweet and others in the church are clearly New Age sympathizers, their unbiblical New Age teachings remain uncontested in a church that doesn't seem to understand what is going on. Trying to use science to prove something that is not true—God "in" everything—is just another clever device being used by Satan to deceive the church:

> Laying up in store for themselves a good foundation against the time to come, that they may lay hold on eternal life. O Timothy, keep that which is committed to thy trust, avoiding profane and vain babblings, and oppositions of science falsely so called: Which some professing have erred concerning the faith. (1 Timothy 6:19-21)

10) The Planetary Pentecost—A False Last Days Revival

As part of the New Age movement, we believed we would be part of a global revival to bring about world peace. The New Age "Christ" states, and we believed, that Armageddon does not *have* to happen—that there is an "alternative to Armageddon" that he calls the "Planetary Pentecost."[23] It is described as an ultimate revival for the world and the church. It would engender everyone's hope for "God's Dream" for world peace. But there is no alternative to prophecy, and the Book of Revelation is presented as direct prophecy from Jesus Christ (Revelation 1:1-3).

The Book of Revelation does not mention any *true* worldwide revival taking place in the latter times. Rather it appears there will be a *false* New Age revival that will bring on a *false* New Age "Christ" and a *false* New Age peace. But in the end, "God's

Dream" will become a New Age nightmare. They will say peace, but there will be no peace until the true Christ—Jesus Christ—actually returns. Dangling the possibility of world peace through a false planetary revival that will include an apostate "church," this Planetary Pentecost is perhaps one of Satan's cruellest devices.

> For when they shall say, Peace and safety; then sudden destruction cometh upon them, as travail upon a woman with child; and they shall not escape. (1 Thessalonians 5:3)

SAVED

FOR MY WIFE, Joy, and I, the end of our New Age involvement came abruptly. Suddenly having to deal with what seemed to be an evil presence, yet holding to our New Age belief that evil was not real, we were at a loss in how to deal with our situation. We tried everything we had learned from our New Age teachings, and nothing worked.

In the midst of what we now know to have been spiritual warfare coming through a particular individual who had been a client of Joy's holistic massage practice, I found Johanna Michaelsen's Christian book *The Beautiful Side of Evil* in the New Age section of a secular bookstore. The reality of evil and Jesus' victory over evil was clearly presented. The next time the evil presence reappeared, I put what I had learned from Johanna's book to use. Addressing this presence I prayed and commanded in the name of Jesus Christ that it leave—and it did! All the Scriptures in Johanna's book about Jesus' victory on the Cross of Calvary and His defeat of sin, evil, death, and the Devil began to click in.

After surrendering our lives to the Lord, we knew we had a responsibility to warn as many people as possible about the New Age and its dangerous deception. What we discovered over time was that the same spiritual devices that had seduced us into accepting New Age teachings were seriously seducing the church as well.

Through the years, we have watched as the situation has grown "worse and worse"—just as Scripture said it would (2 Timothy 3:13). The line distinguishing the differences between the New Age/New Spirituality and a growing apostate church has been broken down and seriously breeched. The great deception is upon us. May the Lord have mercy on us all!

> Let thy mercy, O Lord, be upon us, according as we hope in thee. (Psalm 33:22)

2

THE NEW NARRATIVE

> And the Lord said, Behold, the people is one, and they have all one language; and this they begin to do: and now nothing will be restrained from them, which they have imagined to do. (Genesis 11:6)

Many terms, some of them previously discussed but worth repeating, are being used by both the New Age/New Spirituality and the Christian church. As these terms and their meanings merge together, a New Gospel and a New Worldview are becoming more and more apparent. This New Gospel/New Spirituality has been euphemistically described as a "fresh" "new narrative." It is being called "God's Dream" for a struggling and hurting world. The following are some of the key terms and concepts that provide the semantic undergirding for this New Worldview and emerging New World Religion.

OVERLAPPING TERMS

A Course in Miracles. Commonly referred to as the New Age "Bible," this voluminous work was first published in 1975. It was alleged to be "new revelation" channeled from Jesus Himself. However, all this new revelation and all of the *Course* teachings contradict every major doctrine in the Bible.

The *Course* was enthusiastically endorsed by many New Age leaders, including Gerald Jampolsky, Marianne Williamson, Wayne Dyer, and Oprah Winfrey. This heretical set of false teachings also found its way into the Christian church through undiscerning church leaders like the late Robert Schuller.

Alchemy. This is an occult New Age term that has become part of the language of today's church. *Webster's Dictionary* includes alchemy in its definition of the word occult. *Webster's* also lists occultism as one of the synonyms for alchemy, along with sorcery, witchcraft, magic, wizardry, necromancy, and devilry. Yet in *Jesus Calling*, Sarah Young's "Jesus" says, "I can glean joy out of sorrow, Peace out of adversity. Only a Friend who is also the King of kings could accomplish this divine alchemy."[1] This is a perfect example of how occult words have crossed over into the church as they create a mystical vocabulary for the rapidly emerging One World Religion.

Alternative to Armageddon. The New Age/New Spirituality Christ teaches there is an "alternative" to Armageddon. This false Christ says that Armageddon does not *have* to happen. Rather, he states that humanity can choose to have a peaceful or a violent future—that it is completely up to us. This false Christ denies that the Book of Revelation is prophecy. However, in Revelation 1:3, Jesus states that all the events described in Revelation *are* prophecy. These prophetic events are not presented as possibilities or probabilities. They *will* come to pass. And among these prophetic events are the coming of Antichrist and the Battle of Armageddon. God is not being pessimistic or negative with these prophetic warnings. He is just telling it as it is and how it will be. Yet false teachers in the world and in the church are saying that the future is a blank slate and that nobody, not even God, knows what the future will be. However, Scripture assures us that God has seen the end from the beginning: "Declaring the end from the beginning, and from ancient times the things that are not yet done, saying, My counsel shall stand" (Isaiah 46:10).

As Above, So Below. This term is well known in occult New Age/New Spirituality circles, as well as in Satanism and witchcraft. "As above, so below" is universally acknowledged by these occultists to be the key to all magic and spiritual mysteries. It means that God is "in" everyone and everything—both in Heaven and on Earth. However, the Bible is clear that God is separate from His creation and is not "in" everyone and everything. Yet, this Hermetic occult phrase is presented as part of the Lord's Prayer in Eugene Peterson's *Message* paraphrase of the Bible, and it is actually spoken by Peterson's "Jesus." Instead of "in earth as it is in heaven," Peterson inserts the occult phrase "as above, so below." Over twenty years ago, Peterson was confronted about his use of this mystical, magical, New Age term in *The Message.* He said if he had known it was an occult/New Age phrase, he never would have used it. But he apparently cared so little about the overlapping implications of this occult term that he never had it removed, and it still remains in *The Message* today.

At-one-ment. At-one-ment is a clever New Age play on both the word and biblical concept of atonement. The Bible teaches that believers become one with Jesus Christ through their faith in His sacrificial death on the Cross of Calvary—otherwise known as the atonement. But the New Age/New Spirituality at-one-ment teaches that everyone is already "One" in Christ because Christ is said to be "in" everyone and everything. People save themselves—according to the New Age/New Spirituality—not by believing in Jesus' atoning death and sacrifice, but by believing in the "God" and "Christ" that are already within them (i.e.,

"Christ consciousness"). Thus, New Age at-one-ment bypasses the Cross as it redirects people to "go within" to the "God within." Because church leaders do not point out the overlapping New Age implications of the term at-one-ment, a deceived church is not only using this same hyphenated version of the term itself but could one day accept its heretical meaning.

Awaken/Awakening. In the New Age/New Spirituality, awaken usually means to meditate on, and "awaken" to the "God within"—the God who is said to be "in" everyone and everything. But there is no such "God within." Church leaders hope for a revival that will be a great "awakening" to the historic God and Christ of the Bible. However, they do not warn about the New Age twisting of the term "awakening." Apparently, they don't see how easily the church meaning could shift and overlap with the New Age/New Spirituality meaning in the extremely deceptive days to come.

Change Agent. Many New Age *and* Christian leaders describe themselves as change agents.[2] These change agents are in the process of changing many things—including key spiritual teachings and concepts. As a result, both camps are slowly transforming the Bible's Gospel of Jesus Christ to the New Age/New Gospel of a false Christ. It is because of these change agents and their overlapping vocabulary that a "new narrative" is emerging. The Bible specifically warns to "meddle not with them that are given to change" (Proverbs 24:21).

Change History. Change history is an overlapping term used by both New Age and church leaders. It expresses their belief that future spiritual change will be so great that it will alter and forever change history—change *His* story. In short, the mission of today's change agents is to change the "old" Gospel story to a "new" gospel story—"a new narrative"—that will be compatible with other religions and with the coming One World Religion.

Christ. The word Christ, in and by itself, means "anointed one," "Messiah." There is the true Christ—Jesus Christ—but Scripture warns there have been and will be many false Christs. The ultimate false Christ will be the Antichrist. The Bible reveals that one day he will deceive the whole world into believing that *he*—not Jesus Christ—is the true Christ. In these deceptive days in which we live, with so much New Age/New Spirituality permeating our society and the church, we should do more than use the single word Christ to describe Jesus. We should specify His whole name and title—Jesus Christ. Why? Because in the New Age/New Spirituality the word "Christ" is an overlapping term used to signify the false New Age Christ who is "in" everyone and everything.

Christ Within/Christ-Self/Christ Consciousness. The Christ within/Christ-Self is a false New Age/New Spirituality concept stating that Christ naturally dwells within every person. People are said to have Christ consciousness when they "awaken" to the reality of their "at-one-ment" with their Christ within—their Christ-Self.

Co-create. Co-create is the New Age/New Spirituality notion that as people recognize they are "God," they can then co-create with God. But we are not God nor a part of God. Sadly, this idea that we can co-create with God has made its way into the church through books like *Jesus Calling*. Author Sarah Young's "Jesus" says, "I, the Creator of the universe, have deigned to co-create with you."[3] The Bible makes it clear that we are "labourers together with God"—not co-creators (1 Corinthians 3:9).

Convergence. Convergence is a term used by both New Age/ New Spirituality and Christian leaders. It signifies the coming together of two or more separate entities. Spiritually, it can herald the coming together of different faith traditions as they gradually converge to form a One World Religion. Teilhard de Chardin (1881-1955), the paleontologist/theologian who is frequently referred to as the "Father of the New Age movement," stated: "A general convergence of religions upon a universal Christ who fundamentally satisfies them all: that seems to me the only possible conversion of the world, and the only form in which a religion of the future can be conceived."[4] It should be noted that many church leaders refer positively to the New Age Teilhard de Chardin.

Cosmic Christ. Cosmic Christ is a mystical reference to the universal Christ of the New Age/New Spirituality. The Cosmic Christ is *not* Jesus Christ. The Cosmic Christ is the one who will oversee the coming One World Religion and who is "in" everyone and everything. Sadly, the term Cosmic Christ is being used by undiscerning church leaders.

Day of Declaration. There will be a day when the Antichrist tells the world that *he*—not Jesus Christ—is "the Christ." The Antichrist will most likely explain that mistaking Jesus as the Christ has caused much tragedy and confusion in the world and in the church. He will state that he is returning to "set things right" by correcting the mistaken belief that Jesus is the Christ. From the perspective of the New Age/New Spirituality/New World Religion, the Day of Declaration is a glorious day.

Emergence. The term emergence is presently used by New Age followers to signify the emergence of their New Age/New

Spirituality and the emergence of their New Age Christ. The word has also been used by undiscerning church leaders to describe an emerging "New Christianity." This emergent church, now calling itself among other names—progressive Christianity—is a major deceptive force as it gradually merges and converges into a New Spirituality/New Christianity that will one day become part of the New World Religion.

Force. In New Age teachings, the word force is used as a substitute for the word God and is said to be an energy force that pervades and interpenetrates all creation. This definition has been articulated by the New Age/New Spirituality Christ through channelers like the late New Age leader Barbara Marx Hubbard. Sounding much like the deceptive phenomenon of Holy Laughter, this false Christ says that one day his "joy of the force" will "flood" the body of mankind when he comes to save planet Earth. "May the Force be with you" was no idle comment in the movie *Star Wars*. Not surprisingly, the indiscriminate use of the word force has already entered the church through undiscerning church leaders like Robert Schuller and Rick Warren.[5] It is important to remember that the prophet Daniel makes mention of the "God of forces" in conjunction with Antichrist (Daniel 11:38).

Fractal. *Webster's Dictionary* defines a fractal as "any of various extremely irregular curves or shapes for which any suitably chosen part is similar in shape to a given larger or smaller part when magnified or reduced to the same size." Commonly referred to in relation to quantum physics and quantum spirituality, fractals have entered the church through crossover books like *The Shack*. Fractals are used to try and prove that when any form of creation is broken down, the fractal part is always a part of the creative "force" referred to as God. Thus, fractals are presented as a core tenet of the "new science" that is falsely claiming that God is "in" everyone and everything and therefore "All is One."

Fresh. Describing something as "fresh" carries with it the insinuation that something is "new" and "different" and even exciting. This overlapping term can mean that something considered "old"—like the Bible—can be reinvigorated and made to seem "new"—as in New Age/New Christianity/New Spirituality. The word fresh has been used by both New Age and church leaders to infer that biblical Christianity is somehow lacking and that something "fresh" needs to be added. Scripture is quick to remind us that a little leaven—something inappropriately "fresh"—could conceivably leaven the whole church into something "new" and "different"—like a New Age/New Spirituality (Galatians 5:7-9).

God's Dream. God's Dream is yet another overlapping occult New Age term that can be traced as far back as the early 1900s. It was referenced in a New Age magazine that was published for those interested in the occult and the coming of the New Age Christ.[6] In reality, God's Dream is a devilish scheme devised by our Spiritual Adversary to meld together two irreconcilable worldviews—the New Age/New Spirituality and biblical Christianity. Pastors Robert Schuller and Rick Warren have been chiefly responsible for popularizing this New Age term within the church. In fact, Rick Warren calls his highly promoted Peace Plan—"God's Dream for You and the World." While many New Age and church leaders now use this term, it cannot be found anywhere in the Bible. The prophet Jeremiah warned about false dreams like God's Dream that come from false prophets and not from God (Jeremiah 23:32, also see Deuteronomy 13:1-4).

Guided Visualization. Guided visualization (or guided meditation) is an occult New Age practice commonly used in today's church as modeled by Sarah Young in *Jesus Calling*. However, we are not to visualize Jesus or "a golden light"[7] or anything else as part of our prayer, meditation, or spiritual practice. The demonic realm is only too glad to enter into the visualization and become a part of it. This unscriptural activity can ultimately lead to great deception and spiritual delusion.

Hatred/Hater. In the New Age/New Spirituality scheme of things, a hater is defined as anyone who does not subscribe to the "Doctrine of Oneness"—the teaching that God is "in" everyone and everything. The channeled New Age Christ explicitly states that hatred is "begotten"—caused by—those who believe in "Separation"[8]—those who believe that God is *not* "in" everyone and everything. Thus, biblical believers are defined as "haters" and their Christian beliefs as "hateful."

Holy Laughter. Holy Laughter is a deceptive spiritual phenomenon. Frequently described as a powerful "move of God," it swept through the church in the 1990s. Still present today, it is quite capable of becoming a major *force* again. With no biblical precedent, and no scriptural justification for its manifestation, people experiencing Holy Laughter often break into long uncontrollable fits of laughter. Many of them have found themselves involuntarily shaking, jerking, roaring, yelling, screaming, and even making animal noises as they fall to the floor. Incredibly, people were convinced that Holy Laughter was proof that God was bringing revival to a spiritually depleted church that needed "a fresh touch." It is important to note that Holy Laughter bears a strong resemblance to the "joy of the force" that the false New Age Christ said would "flood" humanity during what he calls his "Planetary Pentecost." He also referred to this Planetary Pentecostal experience as the "Planetary Smile." Holy Laughter resembles a similarly deceptive phenomenon in other religions, such as the ecstatic "kriyas" that manifest after a guru's touch in Hinduism and is called Shaktipat.

Immanent/Immanence. This is the metaphysical/New Age way of saying that God is "in" everyone and everything. Formerly, the church used this term to signify that God was omnipresent throughout His creation. Now the New Age/New Spirituality definition is superseding this previous definition in the church. For example, one popular televangelist, watched by millions, proclaimed that God was not only "transcendent" but also "immanent." He then defined what he meant by immanent by saying "God is alive and he is in every single human being."[9]

Lie of Separation. The alleged "Lie of Separation" is part of the New Age/New Narrative. It warns that because biblical Christianity teaches that God and creation are separate, Christianity is therefore guilty of the "Lie of Separation" by teaching that God is not "in" everyone and everything. But this "Lie of Separation" is actually a lie in and by itself. Most believers are unaware that this New Age "Lie of Separation" has already entered the church in a number of ways, such as in best-selling *Shack* author William Paul Young's twenty-part television series *Restoring the Shack.* In one particular segment, Young describes a vision that a pastor/friend allegedly had from God. In recounting the vision, Young quotes "God" specifically warning about the "lie of separation." He further quotes "God" as saying that "the western world has convinced itself that it has separated itself from God. There has never been separation. That is absolutely a myth."[10] And millions of TBN viewers heard this lie about the "lie of separation" that is actively preparing the world and the church for a New Age/New Spirituality/New World Religion.

Light–bearer. An online thesaurus lists the following synonyms for the term light-bearer—Lucifer, Beelzebub, Prince of Darkness, and Tempter. In fact, the New Age Theosophical Society published a monthly journal in the late 1800s titled *Lucifer* that featured a front cover banner that read, "The Light-bearer is the Morning Star or Lucifer."[11] And while this term cannot be found anywhere in the Bible, Sarah Young and Eugene Peterson put this occult/New Age term in their best-selling books, *Jesus Calling* and *The Message* respectively. This is just one more example of the overlapping language that is merging the church and the New Age/New Spirituality together as "One."

Maitreya. Maitreya is the name of a false Christ figure who claims that *he*—not Jesus Christ—is "the Christ." For decades his spokesman and channel was the Scottish occultist Benjamin Creme. While Creme and some of Maitreya's other spokesmen have passed away, Maitreya is said to still be around, waiting in the wings to make his Day of Declaration and world appearance. His Share International organization is active and continues to proclaim the continual "emergence" of this false Christ figure. Maitreya serves not only as a possible prototype for Antichrist but remains a viable candidate for the position himself.

Master Jesus. The New Age/New Spirituality teaches that Jesus Christ was not "Lord" and "Christ" but rather a disciple of "the Christ." Jesus is not referred to as Jesus Christ but rather as the "Master Jesus." But while the disciples in the Bible did refer to Jesus as Master, it was always in conjunction with His also being called Lord and Christ. Nowhere in the Bible is Jesus Christ ever called just the Master Jesus. In the coming New World Religion, the Master Jesus is already being described as the one who will lead the Christian church from Rome in its adoration and worship of "the Christ." However, this "Christ" would, in reality, be the Antichrist. Thus, the New Age/New Spirituality "Christ" will be the head of all religions—including an apostate Christianity—in his New World Religion. The Bible warns us not to fall for "another Jesus," like the "Master Jesus," who will be a clever imposter (2 Corinthians 11:4), and it warns us not to be deceived by a false Christ who will pretend to be Christ (Matthew 24:3-5).

Masters of Wisdom. The false New Age Christ Maitreya's teachings state that when "the Christ" comes and reveals himself, he will be accompanied by his "Masters of Wisdom" (including the "Master Jesus"). This is an obvious spiritual counterfeit of 2 Thessalonians 1:7-10 that says when Jesus Christ returns, He will come with His "mighty angels"—not with these alleged Masters of Wisdom.

Meant to Be. The term "meant to be" describes how circumstances can converge in such a way as to make it look like it was all divinely planned. Many New Agers and undiscerning Christians automatically assume that any unique convergence of events are "meant to be" from God. And while God can certainly arrange converging circumstances, so can the evil spirit realm. When "meant to be" circumstances present themselves, the obvious question should be—"meant to be" by *whom*?

Necromancy. Necromancy is interacting with the dead and is specifically warned about in the Bible. People who engage in this practice—as well as the practice itself—are described as an "abomination unto the Lord" (Deuteronomy 18:10-12). In Jesus' account of the Rich Man and Lazarus, He specifically warns that *no one* will be sent from the dead to "testify" or interact in any way with people on Earth (Luke 16:19-31). While necromancy is commonly practiced by channelers, psychics, and other occultists, this forbidden practice has been introduced into the church by a prominent pastor who wrote a book that describes how he and his family are meeting and interacting with their deceased son.[12]

New Age Movement. What used to be called "metaphysical" or "occult" has become popularly known in the last fifty or so years as the New Age movement. It is an alternate worldview that directly contradicts the teachings of the Bible. It heralds the coming of a New Age Christ—who is not Jesus Christ—and the coming of a New Spirituality/New World Religion. Sorcery, magic, psychic readings, interacting with the dead, channeling, meditation, Reiki, angel worship, witchcraft, astrology, Tarot cards, New Thought and the whole gamut of occult practices, all fall under this New Age umbrella. But as New Age teachings were exposed and warned about in the 1980s and 1990s, the New Age cleverly shed its name and became the New Spirituality. The false teachings of this New Age/New Spirituality have invaded and dulled the church in a number of ways through its best-selling books, overlapping language, and deceptive spiritual experiences through practices like contemplative prayer.

New Gospel. The New Gospel is not the Gospel of Jesus Christ. It is the "new narrative" of a New Spirituality that has become the foundation of what will become the Antichrist's New World Religion. The New Gospel falsely proclaims that man must "awaken" to the "God," "Christ," and "Holy Spirit" that is reputedly "in" everyone and everything. In contrast, the Bible makes it clear that man and God are not "in" everyone and everything. Scripture teaches that mankind is separated from God because of man's sin and that the "wages of sin is death" (Romans 6:23). The true Gospel offers us salvation from that penalty of sin. Romans 10:9-10 says, "If thou shalt confess with thy mouth the Lord Jesus, and shalt believe in thine heart that God hath raised him from the dead, thou shalt be saved. For with the heart man believeth unto righteousness; and with the mouth confession is made unto salvation."

New Light. New Light is an overlapping New Age term that is being used favorably by some in the church.

New Narrative. The new narrative is a term that is commonly used today, both in the world and in the church. It is an overlapping term that seems to give a "fresh" take on the Bible and on spiritual things in general. The new spiritual narrative taking shape in the world and in the church does not hold to biblical truth. As a result, it undermines the true Gospel story as it becomes a new gospel story that is, in reality, a "cunningly devised fable" (2 Peter 1:16).

New Reformation (Re–formation). New Reformation is a term being used and abused by both church and New Age leaders. A New Reformation implies the need to change things. The very term opens the door to changing biblical doctrine and scriptural teachings in general. Over the years, pastors like Robert Schuller and Rick Warren have frequently pushed for a New Reformation. The channeled New Age "God" likes this idea of a New Reformation and actually praised Schuller for his use of the term.[13] The reason the New Age "God" likes this is because he is already in the process of re-forming the Christian faith to conform to his coming New World Religion.

New Revelation. New revelation can refer to new spiritual information that has allegedly been given to mankind by "God," "Jesus," the "Holy Spirit," channelers, psychics, angels, deceased loved ones, and other various sources. *A Course in Miracles*, as already noted, was supposedly channeled from "Jesus." New revelation attempts to re-form and transform biblical Christianity into a New Age/New Christianity. In the guise of new revelation, every major biblical doctrine is being turned upside down. These new revelations are superseding and taking precedence over the Bible as they purport to clarify what God wants us to believe and follow today. However, these new revelations are being used to deceive both the world and the church with their false teachings and misinformation.

New Science. There is much talk about "new science" and a new way of looking at God and life. This new science attempts to use the spiritualization of quantum physics—a quantum spirituality—to present a New Age/New Spirituality to the world and the church. However, in regard to this new science, with its new revelations, we are reminded there is "no new thing under the sun" that will contradict what is written in the Holy Bible (Ecclesiastes 1:9).

New Spirituality. During the 1990s, when the New Age movement was being thoroughly exposed, it reinvented and renamed itself the New Spirituality. Over the years a number of church leaders have used this same term to describe their updated and re-formed version of Christianity as they wittingly, or unwittingly, help to merge the church with the New Age/New Gospel/New Spirituality.

New Thought. The late New Age researcher Ray Yungen wrote that "one of the most conventional and acceptable elements of the New Age is New Thought."[14] With its emphasis on positive thinking, New Thought tries to distance itself from the New Age—but it is squarely under the occult umbrella of the New Age. New Thought leader Eric Butterworth's website has described him as a "New Age Pioneer."[15] Countless Unity churches describe themselves as New Thought, yet they endorse, practice, and even sell the channeled New Age teachings of *A Course in Miracles.*

Oneness vs. Separation. The Bible makes it clear that God and His creation are distinct and separate. We are born again when we recognize and accept Jesus Christ's sacrificial death on the Cross of Calvary. After this profession and confession of Jesus Christ, the Holy Spirit is sent to reside in the believer so the believer is now *one* "in" Christ (Galatians 3:26-28), and Christ is now "in" him (Colossians 1:27). Only *then* is being "one" in Christ biblically correct. New Age teachings, on the other hand, argue that *everyone* is "One" because "God" and "Christ" are *already* "in" everyone and everything.

Overshadow. Overshadow is a term used in Luke 1:35 when the angel Gabriel spoke to Mary and told her that the Holy Ghost would "overshadow" her. However, the term overshadow has been deceptively incorporated into the New Age/New Spirituality narrative. The false Christ of the New Spirituality falsely asserts that he is the *real* Christ and that he simply overshadowed and worked through the "Master Jesus" in the first century. In other words, this antichrist figure is saying that *he* is "the Christ" and that Jesus is not. He says that when he and the "Master Jesus" appear together, they will correct this alleged misperception of Jesus being the Christ by "setting all things right."

Panentheism. Panentheism is a term that signifies that God *is* "in" everyone and everything. It is the core doctrine of the New Age/New Spirituality/New Narrative. But it is not biblical, and it is not true.

Pantheism. This term signifies that God is everything. It is also not biblical and not true.

Planetary Pentecost or New Age Revival. The late New Age leader Barbara Marx Hubbard's "Christ"[16] told her that planet Earth is at an evolutionary crossroads, and that the people of the world will have a choice to make. If they "awaken" to their own divinity and align themselves as "One" with God and with each other, there can be a Planetary Pentecost—a Planetary Revival—and the world can be saved. But if people hold onto their belief in biblical "separation," the world could be plunged into darkness and destruction. This false "Christ" explains that with *his* spiritual guidance, most of humanity will choose to evolve and the world will survive as "One." He calls this Planetary Pentecost the "Planetary Birth Experience" and warns that those who continue to believe in the "lie of separation" will have to be eliminated for the good of all.

Planetary Birth Experience. Barbara Marx Hubbard's New Age Christ states that the Planetary Pentecost will lead to a "Planetary Birth Experience." It will be a shared event in the future—an "Instant of Co-operation." This false Christ states that everyone who sees themselves as a part of God, and aligns themselves accordingly, will be mysteriously changed in the "twinkling of an eye" and collectively "born" into a "new creation." The Planetary Birth Experience will be the culmination of the Planetary Pentecost and its false revival. This presentation of a latter-days

Pentecostal-like revival and the purported emergence of this false Christ obviously conflicts with the Bible's true account of the coming of the true Christ.

Planetary Smile. The Planetary Smile is another name given for this New Age/New Spirituality/Planetary Pentecost and its "joy of the force." The term immediately brings to mind, and overlaps with, the ungodly practice of Holy Laughter that has deceived and dulled so many people in the church.

Quantum Leap. According to New Age teachers, a huge spiritual leap will be made to the New World Religion when humanity unites around the belief that they are all "One" because they are all a part of God. This leap will be sudden and profound. And it will be seen as a "quantum leap" because humanity's newfound "Oneness" will allegedly be founded upon new spiritual understandings derived from breakthrough discoveries in quantum physics. Scientists will proclaim that God is an energy force that inhabits and interpenetrates everyone and everything. This universal quantum leap of declaring one's divinity and oneness with God will allegedly produce a Planetary Birth Experience. One day these new understandings may be deceptively described as "one spiritual step for man, and one quantum leap for mankind."

Quantum Spirituality. Certain physicists and self-described "futurists"—both in the New Age movement and today's church—have introduced a quantum approach for a New Spirituality. One professing evangelical church leader wrote a book titled *Quantum Spirituality.*[17] The concept of a quantum spirituality is part of a new narrative that promises to bring an otherwise divided world into harmonic convergence and spiritual "Oneness." Quantum advocates would have us believe that humanity is about to take a quantum leap into a new transformational quantum spirituality that will unify the world and all its religions. They say this is inevitable because this spiritualized quantum physics is "proving" that God is "in" everyone and everything. But God is not "in" everyone and everything. The Bible has warned us in advance about those who "have erred concerning the faith" because of the "oppositions of science falsely so called" (1 Timothy 6:20-21).

Quantum Transformation. New Age quantum proponents describe how the future quantum leap will trigger a Quantum Transformation that will ultimately produce the Planetary Birth Experience. This will occur when everyone becomes part of the Planetary Pentecost as they massively "awaken" to their scientifically "proven" quantum self—the "God within." Leonard Sweet, the church leader who authored *Quantum Spirituality*, introduces this new narrative as "new light" teachings.

Reimagining. The Bible consistently warns about the misuse of one's imagination. Reimagining sounds inventive and even upbeat, but the term is helping to create a New Christianity that is not Christianity at all. The Bible further warns that we must always be about the business of "casting down imaginations, and every high thing that exalteth itself against the knowledge of God, and bringing into captivity every thought [imagined or re-imagined] to the obedience of Christ" (2 Corinthians 10:5).

Reinventing. Reinventing is another overlapping term much like "fresh" and "reimagine." It is an enticing word that makes it easier to accept something that is new and different—like a New Gospel/New Spirituality.

Revolution. *Merriam-Webster Dictionary* defines revolution, in part, as a paradigm shift. It says that a revolution can be "a fundamental change in the way of thinking about or visualizing something: a change of paradigm." New Age leader Marianne Williamson stated, "An underground revolution is sweeping the hearts and minds of the people of the world." She said, "This revolution is a fundamental change of worldview."[18] She also said: "It is time for a huge revolution in our understanding of Christic philosophy, and most particularly in our understanding of Jesus."[19] One emergent church leader similarly stated, "The time has come for a new kind of conversation, a new kind of Christianity, a new kind of revolution."[20] But all this talk about a spiritual revolution is very deceptive because the overlapping vocabulary of a new narrative dangerously draws the world and the church together as "One." However, biblical Christianity has nothing to do with revolution and change. The Bible is sufficient just as it is. Jesus Christ is "the same yesterday, and to day, and for ever" (Hebrews 13:8). And what is God's answer to all this talk about revolution and change? He simply and authoritatively says, "I am the Lord, I change not" (Malachi 3:6).

Selection Process. The false New Age Christ, in describing the Planetary Birth Experience and in professing his love of mankind, nevertheless warns that there will be no place in his New Jerusalem for those who refuse to acknowledge *him* as "the Christ." Thus, he outlines the necessity of a "Selection Process."[21] This process will identify and select out all resistant individuals who refuse to follow him and his New Age/New Spirituality/New World Religion. He describes this Selection Process as a purification process that will eliminate resistant people, such as faithful Christians, through the "shock of a fire."[22] The Bible is quick to warn us not to be surprised by fiery trials like the Selection Process—"Beloved, think it not strange concerning the fiery trial which is to try you, as though some strange thing happened unto you (1 Peter 4:12).

Shift (Paradigm Shift). To shift something is to exchange or replace one thing with another. A paradigm is a philosophical, theoretical, or spiritual framework of any kind. Thus, a paradigm shift in the spiritual realm is to exchange or replace one spiritual framework with another. And that is what our Spiritual Adversary is attempting to do—replace biblical Christianity with a new narrative and a New Spirituality. Both the church and the New Age frequently use the term "shift." The question is, what are we shifting from and what are we shifting to?

Sorcery. Sorcery covers a wide gamut of occult practices that are based in magic and witchcraft. Through the control and assistance of deceptive evil spirits, uplifting spiritual experiences can be produced, false healings accomplished, false miracles manifested, and one's deepest desires being demonically fulfilled. Divination and necromancy are a part of sorcery too. The Bible warns that one day the whole world will be deceived by sorcery (Revelation 18:23). One of the Greek words for sorcery—*pharmakeia*—seems to infer that this global deception will also be caused by mind-altering drugs that would include the delusional and injurious side effects from ceremonial, recreational, and pharmaceutical drug use.

Source. Source is a word used by some in the church but is most particularly used in the New Age/New Spirituality as a substitute for, or in place of, God. A New Age follower might say, "I am going to see a psychic who is able to channel directly from the Source of all things." Or, "the Source made it clear I was not to take that job." It is yet another way of making God more of an energy field rather than a personal Creator.

Spirit Guide. Spirit guides are purported to be benign and beneficial spirits sent to assist and guide people in their daily lives. They can manifest in the guise of angels, departed loved ones, and even "God," "Jesus," and the "Holy Spirit." However, these spiritual impersonators seek to deceive and destroy. There is only one mediator between God and man, and that is Jesus Christ (1 Timothy 2:5).

Universe. In New Age/New Spirituality terms, the "Universe," like the word "Source," is used as a substitute for, or in place of, God. Someone who uses this term might say, "Let's see what the Universe brings me today." Or, "I've asked the Universe to bring me the perfect mate."

Universal Christ. The Universal Christ (or Cosmic Christ) is the false Christ of the New Age/New Spirituality. He is said to be "at One" with all creation, because he is alleged to be "in" everyone and everything. He is said to be the head of every religion and belief system that is being transformed by the overlapping words and concepts of the New Age/New Spirituality/New Narrative. But he is not Christ—he is the Antichrist.

3

Holding Fast to Jesus Christ

> Let us hold fast the profession of our faith without wavering. (Hebrews 10:23)

The Greek word *Christ* is technically a title and means "messiah" or "anointed one." In the first century and throughout the ensuing years, Christ was also understood to be an inherent part of Jesus' name. He declared Himself to be Christ and was consistently referred to in Scripture as Jesus Christ. Nevertheless, there have always been those who have tried to take the title and name of Christ away from Him. There are now a growing number of people calling themselves Christians who are doing the same thing.

Stripping Jesus of his proper name and title obviously leaves the door open for the name of Christ to be given to someone else. Enter the ultimate false Christ—Antichrist. By biblical definition the Antichrist will come in the name of Christ while actually opposing the true Christ—Jesus Christ. The apostle Paul teaches there is a simplicity in Jesus Christ (2 Corinthians 11:3). However, there will also seem to be a simplicity in Antichrist as he deceives and "destroys wonderfully" (Daniel 8:24).

THE TRUE CHRIST—JESUS CHRIST

THE NAME OF Jesus Christ is found throughout the New Testament. His name is above all names (Philippians 2:9) and there is no other name under heaven by which men can be saved (Acts 4:12). He is the way, the truth, and the life, and no one comes to the Father except by Him (John 14:6). Jesus was, is, and forever will be the one and only Christ (Hebrews 13:8). One day every knee will bow and every tongue confess that Jesus Christ is Lord (Philippians 2:10-11). He is the "Lord's Christ" (Luke 2:25-26). All other Christs—most especially Antichrist—are deceivers and imposters. Jesus Christ is our Lord and Savior. He is our shepherd and our wonderful Counselor. He is the one and only Christ—there is no other!

THE FALSE CHRIST—ANTICHRIST

WHILE SCRIPTURE WARNS of many false Christ antichrists, it also warns of a very specific false Christ—the Antichrist. The Bible describes how this forbidding figure will arise one day and deceive the whole world (Revelation 13:1,18:23). The main purpose of this prophesied false Christ is to undermine, supplant, and replace the true Christ—Jesus Christ. Everything the Antichrist does is done to deceive, destroy, and achieve his goal of having everyone worship him as God. This ultimate false Christ will come in his own name (John 5:43) and will convince most of the world that *he*—not Jesus—is the true Christ. But how will he come and how will he deceive the world? The "Master Jesus" scenario offers one very real possibility.

ANTICHRIST AND HIS "MASTER JESUS"

FALSE TEACHERS TEACH that Bible-believing Christians have been completely deceived into believing that Jesus is the Christ.

According to many of these deceptive teachers, the Jesus of the Bible is *a* Christ but he is not *the* Christ. Rather, they teach that he is actually part of a select group of spiritual masters referred to as the "Masters of Wisdom" that represent the world's various religions. Jesus is described as being one of these "Masters of Wisdom." Thus, he is not Jesus Christ, but rather the "Master Jesus." In an extract from *The Titanic and Today's Church,*[1] I describe some of the teachings regarding the "Master Jesus" and his relationship to a false Christ/Antichrist type named Maitreya. The following three-and-a-half pages are from that book:

Maitreya's followers believe he is the emerging "Christ" and "World Teacher" who will return to help us to save ourselves and save our planet; and when enough people call for his "return," he will finally reveal himself on an internationally televised "Day of Declaration." Maitreya spokesman Benjamin Creme stated:

> Maitreya will then be invited by the international media to speak directly to the entire world through the television networks linked together by satellites. On this Day of Declaration, we will see His face on the television screen wherever we have access. The Bible statement "All eyes will see Him" will be fulfilled.[2]

Maitreya's followers have reportedly included many past and present-day world leaders. Former Soviet Union leader Mikhail Gorbachev[3] and the late South African leader Nelson Mandela[4] are two prime examples. Many politicians, celebrities, and spiritual/religious leaders are also said to be secretly devoted to him and his teachings.

One of Maitreya's most deceptive spiritual devices is regarding his teachings about the "Master Jesus." In what would prove to be a cunningly clever counterfeit of Jesus' true return with His "mighty angels" (2 Thessalonians 1:7), Maitreya teaches that when he—Maitreya—comes as "the Christ," twelve disciples—his "Masters of Wisdom"—will also appear with him. Some of these "Masters" are said to already be physically present and active in the world under assumed names. Maitreya says that his "Masters of Wisdom" will work with him to teach humanity the "New Truth"[5] and the "new way"[6] of seeing God in the coming "New Age."[7] He said, "They stand ready to greet the dawn of that New Age which beckons all into divinity."[8]

Benjamin Creme, again speaking for Maitreya, stated that one of the spiritual "Masters" who will "return" with Maitreya is the "Master Jesus." This "Master Jesus" is not described as the Christ, but rather as a "disciple" of Maitreya "the Christ." Maitreya is said to be the only person occupying the "office" of Christ and that he has occupied this "office" for over 2600 years. Creme alleges that it was Maitreya "the Christ" who overshadowed and worked through "the man" Jesus in Palestine back in the first century. Creme explained:

> In the esoteric tradition, the Christ is not the name of an individual but of an Office in the Hierarchy. The present holder of that Office, the Lord Maitreya, has held it for 2,600 years, and manifested in Palestine through His Disciple, Jesus, by the occult method of overshadowing, the most frequent form used for the manifestation of Avatars. He has never left the world, but for 2,000 years has waited and planned for this immediate future time, training His Disciples, and preparing Himself for the awesome task which awaits Him. He has made it known that this time, He Himself will come.[9]

In other words, Maitreya's "Master Jesus" is not the Lord, and he is not the Christ. He is a spiritual "Master" and "Master" only. Maitreya proclaims that he himself is "the Lord" and "the Christ." Benjamin Creme explained that the "Master Jesus" will be serving the "Lord Maitreya" by assuming "the Throne of St. Peter, in Rome." It is there in Rome that the "Master Jesus" will attempt to "reform" and "transform the Christian Churches" "to respond correctly" to the Lord Maitreya and the "new reality" his return creates.

This "Master Jesus" who says he is not "the Christ," is by the Bible's definition a counterfeit Jesus—"another Jesus" (2 Corinthians 11:4). And it is understood that a major part of this counterfeit Jesus' role will be to convince professing Christians they have misunderstood his person and his role and caused great problems in the world as a result. He will make sure that Christians understand that the "Master Jesus" is not the Christ—Maitreya is. Thus, the "Master Jesus" will be in charge of the New Reformation that will educate and reform the Christian churches. Speaking for Maitreya and turning the truth of the Bible upside down, Benjamin Creme stated:

> The Master Jesus is going to reform the Christian churches.[10]

> He is one of the Masters Who will very shortly return to outer work in the world, taking over the Throne of St. Peter, in Rome. He will seek to transform the Christian Churches, in so far as they are flexible enough to respond correctly to the new reality which the return of the Christ and the Masters will create.[11]

Once Maitreya's alleged reign is established, his role is to eventually bring all humanity to the feet of his "Father"—Sanat Kumara. Sanat Kumara is described as "God" and "Lord of the world."[12] It should be noted that Sanat is an anagram for Satan and that the Bible describes Satan as the "god of this world":

> In whom the god of this world hath blinded the minds of them which believe not, lest the light of the glorious gospel of Christ, who is the image of God, should shine unto them. For we preach not ourselves, but Christ Jesus the Lord; and ourselves your servants for Jesus' sake. (2 Corinthians 4:4-5)

Whether or not Maitreya is the actual Antichrist is not the concern here. What is of concern is that his New Age teachings are most likely a template—a blueprint—for the false Christ to come, whoever that may turn out to be. Scripture is very clear that we are not to be ignorant of Satan's devices, especially as he plies the world and the church with his antichrist leaven and false Christs like Maitreya (2 Corinthians 2:11).*

THE NAME AND PERSON OF JESUS CHRIST

SATAN IS DOING everything he can to dethrone "the Lord's Christ" (Luke 2:26), as he deceptively works to crown his own Christ—Antichrist. With so much deception in our midst, believers need to know what the Bible clearly teaches about the true Christ—Jesus Christ. As false teachings gain momentum, we must hold fast to His name and person as we study and continue in His Word.

---

*End of extract from *The Titanic and Today's Church.*

JESUS CHRIST

50 SELECTED VERSES

Jesus Is the Christ

He saith unto them, But whom say ye that I am? And Simon Peter answered and said, Thou art the Christ, the Son of the living God. And Jesus answered and said unto him, Blessed art thou, Simon Barjona: for flesh and blood hath not revealed it unto thee, but my Father which is in heaven. (Matthew 16:15-17)

The Disciples Taught and Preached That Jesus Is the Christ

And daily in the temple, and in every house, they ceased not to teach and preach Jesus Christ. (Acts 5:42)

Scriptures Show That Jesus Is the Christ

And Paul, as his manner was, went in unto them, and three sabbath days reasoned with them out of the scriptures, Opening and alleging, that Christ must needs have suffered, and risen again from the dead; and that this Jesus, whom I preach unto you, is Christ. (Acts 17:2-3)

Jesus Christ Is the Only Lord and Christ

But to us there is but one God, the Father, of whom are all things, and we in him; and one Lord Jesus Christ, by whom are all things, and we by him. (1 Corinthians 8:6)

God Made Jesus Both Lord and Christ

Therefore let all the house of Israel know assuredly, that God hath made that same Jesus, whom ye have crucified, both Lord and Christ. (Acts 2:36)

God Sent Jesus Christ

And this is life eternal, that they might know thee the only true God, and Jesus Christ, whom thou hast sent. (John 17:3)

Jesus Was Born Christ the Lord

Now the birth of Jesus Christ was on this wise: When as his mother Mary was espoused to Joseph, before they came together, she was found with child of the Holy Ghost . . . And she shall bring forth a son, and thou shalt call his name JESUS: for he shall save his people from their sins. (Matthew 1:18, 21)

Jesus Christ Died for Our Sins

Grace be to you and peace from God the Father, and from our Lord Jesus Christ, Who gave himself for our sins, that he might deliver us from this present evil world. (Galatians 1:3-4)

The Gospel Is the Gospel of Jesus Christ

The beginning of the gospel of Jesus Christ, the Son of God. (Mark 1:1)

The Blood of Jesus Christ Cleanses Us From All Sin

But if we walk in the light, as he is in the light, we have fellowship one with another, and the blood of Jesus Christ his Son cleanseth us from all sin. (1 John 1:7)

Believers in Jesus Christ Are Born of God

Whosoever believeth that Jesus is the Christ is born of God. (1 John 5:1)

Those Confessing Jesus Christ Came in the Flesh Are of God

Hereby know ye the Spirit of God: Every spirit that confesseth that Jesus Christ is come in the flesh is of God. (1 John 4:2)

Believers in Jesus Christ Are Alive Unto God

For in that he died, he died unto sin once: but in that he liveth, he liveth unto God. Likewise reckon ye also yourselves to be dead indeed unto sin, but alive unto God through Jesus Christ our Lord. (Romans 6:10-11)

Jesus Christ Is the Only True Foundation

For other foundation can no man lay than that is laid, which is Jesus Christ. (1 Corinthians 3:11)

We Are Redeemed by Jesus Christ

For all have sinned, and come short of the glory of God; Being justified freely by his grace through the redemption that is in Christ Jesus: Whom God hath set forth to be a propitiation through faith in his blood, to declare his righteousness for the remission of sins that are past, through the forbearance of God. (Romans 3:23-25)

We Are Sanctified By Jesus Christ

By the which will we are sanctified through the offering of the body of Jesus Christ once for all. (Hebrews 10:10)

We Are Justified by Jesus Christ

Knowing that a man is not justified by the works of the law, but by the faith of Jesus Christ, even we have believed in Jesus Christ, that we might be justified by the faith of Christ, and not by the works of the law: for by the works of the law shall no flesh be justified. (Galatians 2:16)

We Receive the Atonement Through Jesus Christ

And not only so, but we also joy in God through our Lord Jesus Christ, by whom we have now received the atonement. (Romans 5:11)

We Are God's Children Through Our Faith in Jesus Christ

For ye are all the children of God by faith in Christ Jesus. (Galatians 3:26)

We Are All One in Jesus Christ

There is neither Jew nor Greek, there is neither bond nor free, there is neither male nor female: for ye are all one in Christ Jesus. (Galatians 3:28)

Jesus Christ's Name Is Above All Other Names

Wherefore God also hath highly exalted him, and given him a name which is above every name: That at the name of Jesus every knee should bow, of things in heaven, and things in earth, and things under the earth. And that every tongue should confess that Jesus Christ is Lord, to the glory of God the Father. (Philippians 2:9-11)

We Are Commanded to Believe on the Name of Jesus Christ

And this is his commandment, That we should believe on the name of his Son Jesus Christ, and love one another, as he gave us commandment. (1 John 3:23)

Jesus Christ Was Resurrected

Blessed be the God and Father of our Lord Jesus Christ, which according to his abundant mercy hath begotten us again unto a lively hope by the resurrection of Jesus Christ from the dead. (1 Peter 1:3)

We Have Life Through the Name of Jesus Christ

But these are written, that ye might believe that Jesus is the Christ, the Son of God; and that believing ye might have life through his name. (John 20:31)

Salvation Is Only Through the Name of Jesus Christ

Neither is there salvation in any other [name]: for there is none other name [Jesus Christ] under heaven given among men, whereby we must be saved. (Acts 4:10-12)

We Are to Repent and Be Baptized in the Name of Jesus Christ

Then Peter said unto them, Repent, and be baptized every one of you in the name of Jesus Christ for the remission of sins, and ye shall receive the gift of the Holy Ghost. (Acts 2:38)

We Are to Give Thanks Always in the Name of Jesus Christ

Giving thanks always for all things unto God and the Father in the name of our Lord Jesus Christ. (Ephesians 5:20)

The Name of Jesus Christ Should Be Glorified in Us

Wherefore also we pray always for you, that our God would count you worthy of this calling, and fulfil all the good pleasure of his goodness, and the work of faith with power: That the name of our Lord Jesus Christ may be glorified in you, and ye in him, according to the grace of our God and the Lord Jesus Christ. (2 Thessalonians 1:11-12)

Evil Spirits Are Driven Away by the Name of Jesus Christ

And this did she many days. But Paul, being grieved, turned and said to the spirit, I command thee in the name of Jesus Christ to come out of her. And he came out the same hour. (Acts 16:18)

Walk in the Lord Jesus Christ

As ye have therefore received Christ Jesus the Lord, so walk ye in him. (Colossians 2:6)

Men Have Hazarded Their Lives for the Name of Jesus Christ

Men that have hazarded their lives for the name of our Lord Jesus Christ. (Acts 15:26)

Grace and Truth Come From Jesus Christ

For the law was given by Moses, but grace and truth came by Jesus Christ. (John 1:17)

The Blessing of Abraham Is Upon the Gentiles Through Jesus Christ

That the blessing of Abraham might come on the Gentiles through Jesus Christ; that we might receive the promise of the Spirit through faith. (Galatians 3:14)

Jesus Christ Is the One Mediator Between Men and God

For there is one God, and one mediator between God and men, the man Christ Jesus. (1 Timothy 2:5)

The Promise of Life Is in Jesus Christ

Paul, an apostle of Jesus Christ by the will of God, according to the promise of life which is in Christ Jesus. (2 Timothy 1:1)

God Sent Jesus Christ to Bring Life Eternal

And this is life eternal, that they might know thee the only true God, and Jesus Christ, whom thou hast sent. (John 17:3)

Eternal Life Is a Gift of God Through Jesus Christ

For the wages of sin is death; but the gift of God is eternal life through Jesus Christ our Lord. (Romans 6:23)

We Are to Grow in the Name of Jesus Christ

But grow in grace, and in the knowledge of our Lord and Saviour Jesus Christ. To him be glory both now and for ever. Amen. (2 Peter 3:18)

Peace Comes From Jesus Christ

Therefore being justified by faith, we have peace with God through our Lord Jesus Christ. (Romans 5:1)

The Fruits of Righteousness Are by Jesus Christ

Being filled with the fruits of righteousness, which are by Jesus Christ, unto the glory and praise of God. (Philippians 1:11)

Jesus Christ Is Our Hope

Paul, an apostle of Jesus Christ by the commandment of God our Saviour, and Lord Jesus Christ, which is our hope. (1 Timothy 1:1)

Jesus Christ Supplies All Our Needs

But my God shall supply all your need according to his riches in glory by Christ Jesus. (Philippians 4:19)

Jesus Christ Gives Us the Victory

But thanks be to God, which giveth us the victory through our Lord Jesus Christ. (1 Corinthians 15:57)

The Everlasting Kingdom of Jesus Christ

For so an entrance shall be ministered unto you abundantly into the everlasting kingdom of our Lord and Saviour Jesus Christ. (2 Peter 1:11)

There Is a Simplicity in Jesus Christ

But I fear, lest by any means, as the serpent beguiled Eve through his subtlety, so your minds should be corrupted from the simplicity that is in Christ. For if he that cometh preacheth another Jesus, whom we have not preached, or if ye receive another spirit, which ye have not received, or another gospel, which ye have not accepted, ye might well bear with him. (2 Corinthians 11:3-4)

We Are to Glory in the Cross of Jesus Christ

But God forbid that I should glory, save in the cross of our Lord Jesus Christ, by whom the world is crucified unto me, and I unto the world. (Galatians 6:14)

Jesus Christ Is Coming

Looking for that blessed hope, and the glorious appearing of the great God and our Saviour Jesus Christ; Who gave himself for us, that he might redeem us from all iniquity, and purify unto himself a peculiar people, zealous of good works. (Titus 2:13-14)

Every Tongue Will Confess That Jesus Christ Is Lord

And that every tongue should confess that Jesus Christ is Lord, to the glory of God the Father. (Philippians 2:11)

Jesus Christ Will Judge the Secrets of Men

In the day when God shall judge the secrets of men by Jesus Christ according to my gospel. (Romans 2:16)

Jesus Christ Is the Christ Yesterday, Today and Forever

Jesus Christ the same yesterday, and to day, and for ever. Be not carried about with divers and strange doctrines. (Hebrews 13:8-9)

HOLDING FAST

THE CHURCH IN Pergamos is commended by Jesus Christ for holding fast to His name and not denying their faith even in the midst of fierce persecution and hostility:

> I know thy works and where thou dwellest, even where Satan's seat is: and thou holdest fast my name, and hast not denied my faith, even in those days wherein Antipas was my faithful martyr, who was slain among you, where Satan dwelleth. (Revelation 2:13)

Some Pervert the Gospel of Jesus Christ

I marvel that ye are so soon removed from him that called you into the grace of Christ unto another gospel: Which is not another; but there be some that trouble you, and would pervert the gospel of Christ. (Galatians 1:6-7)

Many Will Come in the Name of Christ

And as he sat upon the mount of Olives, the disciples came unto him privately, saying, Tell us, when shall these things be? and what shall be the sign of thy coming, and of the end of the world? And Jesus answered and said unto them, Take heed that no man deceive you. For many shall come in my name, saying, I am Christ; and shall deceive many. (Matthew 24:3-5)

Deceivers Do Not Confess That Jesus Is the Christ

For many deceivers are entered into the world, who confess not that Jesus Christ is come in the flesh. This is a deceiver and an antichrist. (2 John 1:7)

Some Will Readily Follow Another Jesus

For if he that cometh preacheth another Jesus, whom we have not preached, or if ye receive another spirit, which ye have not received, or another gospel, which ye have not accepted, ye might well bear with him. (2 Corinthians 11:4)

Those Who Deny Jesus Is Christ are Antichrists

Who is a liar but he that denieth that Jesus is the Christ? He is antichrist, that denieth the Father and the Son. Whosoever denieth the Son, the same hath not the Father: (but) he that acknowledgeth the Son hath the Father also. (1 John 2:22-24)

Antichrist Will Come

Little children, it is the last time: and as ye have heard that antichrist shall come, even now are there many antichrists; whereby we know that it is the last time. (1 John 2:18)

Antichrist Will Come in His Own Name

I am come in my Father's name, and ye receive me not: if another shall come in his own name, him ye will receive. (John 5:43)

Antichrist Will Rise Up From Humanity

And I stood upon the sand of the sea, and saw a beast rise up out of the sea, having seven heads and ten horns, and upon his horns ten crowns, and upon his heads the name of blasphemy. (Revelation 13:1)

Antichrist Will Destroy Wonderfully

And his power shall be mighty, but not by his own power: and he shall destroy wonderfully, and shall prosper, and practice, and shall destroy the mighty and the holy people. (Daniel 8:24)

Antichrist Will Deceive All Nations Through Sorcery

And the light of a candle shall shine no more at all in thee; and the voice of the bridegroom and of the bride shall be heard no more at all in thee: for thy merchants were the great men of the earth; for by thy sorceries were all nations deceived. (Revelation 18:23)

Antichrist Will Destroy Many Through Peace

And through his policy also he shall cause craft to prosper in his hand; and he shall magnify himself in his heart, and by peace shall destroy many: he shall also stand up against the Prince of princes; but he shall be broken without hand. (Daniel 8:25)

HOW WILL WE DO?

> If thou hast run with the footmen, and they have wearied thee, then how canst thou contend with horses? and if in the land of peace, wherein thou trustedst, they wearied thee, then how wilt thou do in the swelling of Jordan? (Jeremiah 12:5)

How will we do in perilous times? Will we stand and not faint? One thing is for sure, we will not be overcomers through our own strength. We will need the Lord to perfect His strength in our weakness. He is the one who can keep us from fainting and falling.

> And he said unto me, My grace is sufficient for thee: for my strength is made perfect in weakness. (2 Corinthians 12:9)

> But they that wait upon the LORD shall renew their strength; they shall mount up with wings as eagles; they shall run, and not be weary; and they shall walk, and not faint. (Isaiah 40:31)

> Now unto him that is able to keep you from falling, and to present you faultless before the presence of his glory with exceeding joy. (Jude 1:24)

PRESSING ON

IN 1978, LONG before New Age leaders like Eric Butterworth,[13] Oprah Winfrey, and Marianne Williamson[14] attempted to distance themselves from the term New Age, New Age leader David Spangler explicitly laid out the Antichrist's plan for becoming the universal New Age Christ. Spangler wrote:

> [A]ny old Christ will not do, not if we need to show that we have something better than the mainstream Christian traditions. It must be a cosmic Christ, a universal Christ, a New Age Christ.[15]

Understandably, as New Age leaders and their teachings become more exposed as New Age, they begin to hide themselves and their teachings behind more positive and acceptable terms like New Gospel, New Spirituality, New Worldview, New Christianity, and New Thought. The New Age wants to be known as anything *but* New Age as it continues to reinvent and reimagine biblical Christianity as it paves the way for Antichrist.

To downplay the term New Age is to give false teachers, like Oprah Winfrey and Marianne Williamson, exactly what they want—not to be associated with the very New Age teachings they are bringing into the world and into the church. The New

Age is in fact, an all-inclusive term for what was previously described as the occult. It is active, and it is thriving both in the world and in the church today.

The world is being spiritually manipulated to prepare the way for the Antichrist, to make him credible and to put him in power. It will be explained, and mostly believed, that Christians got it all wrong. That Jesus is not really the Christ. He is just "a" Christ. Someone like the "Master Jesus" will head up the Christian component of the New Age/New World Religion. He will explain how things "really are" and "set all things right." The Antichrist of the New Age will be heralded and recognized as the real Christ. However, as night comes on and the world gets darker, "evil men and seducers shall wax worse and worse, deceiving, and being deceived" (2 Timothy 3:13).

Believers must stand in the truth that the Bible's Jesus is exactly who he says He is—Jesus Christ. We must keep the faith. We must hold fast to the name and person of Jesus Christ as we press on to the higher calling of our Lord.

> I press toward the mark for the prize of the high calling of God in Christ Jesus. (Philippians 3:14)

4

GOD'S TRUTH

I have no greater joy than to hear that my children walk in truth. (3 John 1:4)

In 1940, Ralph Edwards hosted an NBC radio quiz show called *Truth or Consequences*. The show had a simple format. Contestants were presented with a question. If they couldn't answer it correctly—which they almost never did—they suffered consequences that usually proved to be somewhat entertaining and comical in nature.

In 1950, Edwards announced they would broadcast their tenth anniversary program from whatever town or city in America that changed its existing name to Truth or Consequences. The city of Hot Springs, New Mexico, responded by changing their name from Hot Springs to Truth or Consequences. As a result the newly named city hosted the tenth anniversary edition of *Truth or Consequences.*

Ralph Edwards continued to visit the city of Truth or Consequences the first weekend in May for the next fifty years to help celebrate the town's annual "Fiesta." Truth or Consequences, New Mexico, continues to hold "Fiesta" each year, and the celebration includes a dance held in Ralph Edwards Park.[1]

Curiously, the television show used the otherwise serious concept of "truth or consequences" to provide the thematic foundation for their comedy quiz show. The phrase "truth or consequences" would ordinarily suggest a certain degree of solemnity rather than levity. Therefore, the festive atmosphere surrounding the program's novel use of the phrase proved to be somewhat ironic.

To put this into a wider perspective, this could be seen as symptomatic—both then and now—of a society that doesn't take the concept of "truth or consequences" very seriously. In fact, there seems to be a growing apathy and disregard—even in the church—for the consequences of not observing and maintaining truth—most especially God's truth as revealed in the Bible.

LEAVENING THE TRUTH

THE EXPRESSION "GOSPEL truth"—even when used in the secular world—almost always signifies pure, honest, absolute truth. For Bible-believing Christians, "gospel truth" obviously denotes God's absolute truth as contained in His Holy Bible. But today we hear people—both in and out of the church—say there is no such thing as absolute truth. For many, truth has become an abstract concept that we ourselves now define.

Sadly, we live in a time when it's popular to say—"You have your truth, and I have mine." Given that Jesus is "the truth" (John 14:6), "you have your truth, and I have mine" translates into "you have your Jesus, and I have mine." Thus in people's minds, Jesus Christ becomes whatever anyone wants Him to be—not what is necessarily true.

Amongst many believers, it's no longer "a little leaven leaveneth the whole lump" (Galatians 5:9). Rather, it's "I just eat the meat and spit out the bones" as if lies and leaven are no big deal. Or if we don't agree with what has been traditionally accepted as truth, we go along with others who "stretch the truth" or "enlarge the truth" to create a "new truth" that is no truth at all.

Nazi Germany was a good example of this: When big lies were told often enough and convincingly enough, they eventually became accepted as truth. In a slightly more contemporary vein, there was a popular movie in 1994 called *True Lies*. The main character in yet another movie states that he always tells the truth—even when he lies.[2]

New Age leaders would have us believe they have "a great heretical idea" (a lie) that will get humanity out of its present crisis.[3] In their attempt to justify their "lie," as they blaspheme God in the process, these same New Age leaders try to convince us that "All great truth begins as blasphemy."[4] But the blasphemy they propose—"we are all one" because God is "in" everyone and everything—is predicated on their disbelief of God's Truth as revealed in the Holy Bible. In fact, the Bible warns in Romans 1:25 of those "who changed the truth of God into a lie"—a lie they would have us believe is a "new truth" that will save the world.

TRUTH IS OUT OF STYLE?

WE ARE BEING told that the Bible is out of style and outdated—that it's got some good points but it's a two-thousand-year-old book that needs a little changing and some postmodern rearranging. We are further told that spiritual experience is what *really* counts. Because of this, *objectivity* is quickly giving way to *subjectivity*. God's truth is being replaced by what we experience as truth—what we sense, what we feel, what "works" for us.

As a society—and also as a church—we are being deceived into believing that something is true simply because it is what most people believe. As a result, what people agree to believe as truth is triumphing over actual truth. Consequently—and as previously mentioned—literal lies are becoming our "new truths."

Do we, as believers, have a real love of the truth, or do we just want to have our ears tickled by what feels right and seems to be true? The Bible warns:

> There is a way which seemeth right unto a man, but the end thereof are the ways of death. (Proverbs 14:12)

> A wonderful and horrible thing is committed in the land; The prophets prophesy falsely, and the priests bear rule by their means; and my people love to have it so: and what will ye do in the end thereof? (Jeremiah 5:30-31)

> For the time will come when they will not endure sound doctrine; but after their own lusts shall they heap to themselves teachers, having itching ears; And they shall turn away their ears from the truth, and shall be turned unto fables. (2 Timothy 4:3-4)

WHAT IS TRUTH?

THE REASON THE Bible has so much to say about truth is because Jesus Christ *is* the truth. He said "I am the way, the truth, and the life: No man cometh unto the Father, but by me" (John 14:6). Bible-believing Christians trust these words in the Bible because the Bible is—"in truth"—the actual Word of God.

> For this cause also thank we God without ceasing, because, when ye received the word of God which ye heard of us, ye received it not as the word of men, but

> as it is in truth, the word of God, which effectually worketh also in you that believe. (1 Thessalonians 2:13)

The Bible exhorts us to "prove all things" and to "hold fast" to that which is "good"—that which is true (1 Thessalonians 5:21). It commands us to expose the unfruitful works of darkness that oppose truth and to have no fellowship with them (Ephesians 5:11). Scripture warns there are severe consequences for those who—for whatever reason—do not love and protect the truth of God's Word.

BIBLICAL CONSEQUENCES

REVELATION 22:13-15 WARNS that those who "loveth and maketh a lie" will be among those excluded from the city of New Jerusalem:

> I am Alpha and Omega, the beginning and the end, the first and the last. Blessed are they that do his commandments, that they may have right to the tree of life, and may enter in through the gates into the city. For without are dogs, and sorcerers, and whoremongers, and murderers, and idolaters, and whosoever loveth and maketh a lie. (Revelation 22:13-15)

In addition to this warning in Revelation, Jesus made many direct references to Hell. Scripture also warns there will be people who "received not the love of the truth" and "believed not the truth" but "had pleasure in unrighteousness." And because they believe a "lie," they are damned and ultimately "perish" (2 Thessalonians 2:10-12).

> And then shall that Wicked be revealed, whom the Lord shall consume with the spirit of his mouth, and shall destroy with the brightness of his coming: Even him, whose coming is after the working of Satan with all power and signs and lying wonders, And with all deceivableness of unrighteousness *in them that perish; because they received not the love of the truth*, that they might be saved. And for this cause God shall send them strong delusion, that they should believe a lie: That they all *might be damned who believed not the truth*, but had pleasure in unrighteousness. (2 Thessalonians 2:8-12, emphasis added)

It is very evident that there are serious consequences to what we choose to believe and what we choose not to believe regarding the truth of God's Word.

WORLDLY CONSEQUENCES

IN A COURTROOM, witnesses must *tell the truth, the whole truth, and nothing but the truth—so help them God*. There are definite legal consequences for anyone who is not truthful in the court proceedings. Perjury is a punishable offense that can result in heavy fines and possible imprisonment. One "little lie" can totally change the nature of a court case. A "little lie" or a "little leaven" can completely transform something true into something false. The late pastor and evangelist Harry Ironside warned that truth mixed with error is like leaven and is equivalent to *all error*:

> Error is like leaven, of which we read, "A little leaven leaveneth the whole lump." Truth mixed with error is equivalent to all error, except that it is more inno-

> cent looking and, therefore, more dangerous. God hates such a mixture! Any error, or any truth-and-error mixture, calls for definite exposure and repudiation. To condone such is to be unfaithful to God and His Word and treacherous to imperiled souls for whom Christ died.[5]

In today's church, many best-selling "Christian" books contain leavened statements that are patently false when compared to the light of Scripture. But the leaven—error—contained in these books goes largely unchallenged as sales reach into the multiple millions. In today's progressive "Christianity," there seems to be little or no accountability for Christian leaders and authors who present false teachings. The only immediate consequence the authors of these leavened books seem to "suffer" is the attainment of celebrity status and a huge increase in their personal income. What irony. Instead of being held responsible for the leaven contained in their writings, these men and women are rewarded by the church and held in high esteem.

THE HOLY BIBLE: GOD'S LIE DETECTOR

IN THE WORLD, the "truth" of what someone is saying can usually be detected by a polygraph machine—also known as a "lie detector." However, the Christian faith has the ultimate lie detector—the Holy Bible. It is holy because it's the authoritative, inerrant, inspired Word of God. The truth of what people say and teach and do in regard to spiritual matters can be accurately discerned by searching the Scriptures to see if these things are so (Acts 17:11). The Bible rightly defines truth, while at the same time exposes what is false and deceptive. In fact, the truth of God's Word is of such paramount importance to God that He actually magnifies His Word above His own name (Psalm 138:2). God's Word *is* truth (John 17:17) and is the true measure of *all* spiritual things:

> For the word of God is quick, and powerful, and sharper than any twoedged sword, piercing even to the dividing asunder of soul and spirit, and of the joints and marrow, and is a discerner of the thoughts and intents of the heart. (Hebrews 4:12)

> Study to show thyself approved unto God, a workman that needeth not to be ashamed, rightly dividing the word of truth. (2 Timothy 2:15)

> All scripture is given by inspiration of God, and is profitable for doctrine, for reproof, for correction, for instruction in righteousness: That the man of God may be perfect, thoroughly furnished unto all good works. (2 Timothy 3:16-17)

While a genuine Bible remains *the* ultimate lie detector, there are many modern versions that have changed important parts of God's Word. They change it by adding to it, subtracting from it, and watering it down—all for the expressed purpose of making it more "relevant" and "less offensive." However, when the genuine is altered in any way, it is no longer genuine and wholly dependable. Because there are so many new translations and paraphrases, exposing error has become more difficult for the average believer in today's compromised church. And it is unexposed error that ultimately leads to heresy and apostasy.

THE RIGHT HAND OF FALSEHOOD

> Rid me, and deliver me from the hand of strange children, whose mouth speaketh vanity, and their right hand is a right hand of falsehood. (Psalm 144:11)

GALATIANS 2:9 DESCRIBES what is referred to as the right hand of fellowship. In the Bible, the right hand of God generally refers to His power and authority and righteousness. For example, the right hand of God is "exalted" (Psalm 118:16). God "saves" those who put their trust in Him by His right hand (Psalm 17:7). Jesus sits on the right hand of "the power of God" (Luke 22:69). God upholds with the right hand of His "righteousness" (Isaiah 41:10). The right hand of fellowship is based in that power and authority and truth. However, Psalm 144 warns of the hand of "strange children" who extend the "right hand of falsehood." The right hand of falsehood may appear to be the right hand of fellowship, but it is not. It is the kind of deception the Bible warns us to watch out for.

Jesus warns of those who draw near to Him with their mouth, but their hearts are far from Him (Matthew 15:8). Tragically, insistence on truth has taken a back seat to compromise in today's church in its quest for agreement and unity. But truth compromised for the sake of unity is not God's unity at all. Division caused by truth is far better than unity that is based on the right hand of falsehood. Proclaiming "Lord, Lord," and reciting John 14:6 does not legitimize leaven and false teachings. Truth combined with error is, indeed, an ungodly mixture. Half of the truth is still a lie. "Ye cannot drink the cup of the Lord, and the cup of devils" (1 Corinthians 10:21). The right hand of fellowship does not unite and shake hands with the right hand of falsehood.

Because a love of the truth is perishing in the land and in the church, it is imperative that we take a look at what the Bible says about truth—how we must love it and keep it and hold it in the highest regard.

Bible Teachings on Truth

50 SELECTED VERSES

Our God Is a God of Truth

He is the Rock, his work is perfect: for all his ways are judgment: a God of truth and without iniquity, just and right is he. (Deuteronomy 32:4)

All God's Works Are Done in Truth

For the word of the Lord is right; and all his works are done in truth. (Psalm 33:4)

God's Law Is Truth

Thy righteousness is an everlasting righteousness, and thy law is the truth. (Psalm 119:142)

All God's Commandments Are Done in Truth

The works of his hands are verity and judgment; all his commandments are sure. They stand fast for ever and ever, and are done in truth and uprightness. (Psalm 111:7-8)

God's Word Is Truth

Sanctify them through thy truth: thy word is truth. (John 17:17)

God's Word Is—in Truth—the Word of God

For this cause also thank we God without ceasing, because, when ye received the word of God which ye heard of us, ye received it not as the word of men, but as it is in truth, the word of God, which effectually worketh also in you that believe. (1Thessalonians 2:13)

God Desires for All Men to Be Saved and Come to a Knowledge of the Truth

Who will have all men to be saved, and to come unto the knowledge of the truth. (1Timothy 2:4)

Jesus Christ Brought Grace and Truth

For the law was given by Moses, but grace and truth came by Jesus Christ. (John 1:17)

Jesus Christ Is the Truth

Jesus saith unto him, I am the way, the truth, and the life: no man cometh unto the Father, but by me. (John 14:6)

God's Word Is the Gospel Truth

For the hope which is laid up for you in heaven, whereof ye heard before in the word of the truth of the gospel. (Colossians 1:5)

We Are to Desire Truth in Our Innermost Being

Behold, thou desirest truth in the inward parts: and in the hidden part thou shalt make me to know wisdom. (Psalm 51:6)

The Lord Is Close to All Those Who Call Upon Him in Truth

The LORD is nigh unto all them that call upon him, to all that call upon him in truth. (Psalm 145:18)

The Holy Spirit of Truth Is Sent to Believers and Abides With Them Forever

And I will pray the Father, and he shall give you another Comforter, that he may abide with you for ever; Even the Spirit of truth; whom the world cannot receive, because it seeth him not, neither knoweth him: but ye know him; for he dwelleth with you, and shall be in you. I will not leave you comfortless: I will come to you. (John 14:16-18)

The Holy Spirit Guides All Believers Into the Truth

Howbeit when he, the Spirit of truth, is come, he will guide you into all truth: for he shall not speak of himself; but whatsoever he shall hear, that shall he speak: and he will show you things to come. (John 16:13)

God Is Plenteous in His Mercy and Truth

But thou, O Lord, art a God full of compassion, and gracious, longsuffering, and plenteous in mercy and truth. (Psalm 86:15)

We Are to Hold Fast to Mercy and Truth

Let not mercy and truth forsake thee: bind them about thy neck; write them upon the table of thine heart: So shalt thou find favour and good understanding in the sight of God and man. (Proverbs 3:3-4)

We Are to Speak Truth From the Heart

LORD, who shall abide in thy tabernacle? who shall dwell in thy holy hill? He that walketh uprightly, and worketh righteousness, and speaketh the truth in his heart. (Psalm 15:1-2)

We Are to Love Each Other in the Truth

The elder unto the elect lady and her children, whom I love in the truth; and not I only, but also all they that have known the truth; For the truth's sake, which dwelleth in us, and shall be with us for ever. (2 John1:1-2)

We Are to Speak the Truth in Love

That we henceforth be no more children, tossed to and fro, and carried about with every wind of doctrine, by the sleight of men, and cunning craftiness, whereby they lie in wait to deceive; But speaking the truth in love, may grow up into him in all things, which is the head, even Christ. (Ephesians 4:14-15)

We Are to Love in Deed and Truth

My little children, let us not love in word, neither in tongue; but in deed and in truth. (1 John 3:18)

We Are to Worship God in Spirit and in Truth

God is a Spirit: and they that worship him must worship him in spirit and in truth. (John 4:24)

We Are to Serve the Lord in Sincerity and Truth

Now therefore fear the LORD, and serve him in sincerity and in truth. (Joshua 24:14)

We Are to Study and Rightly Divide the Word of Truth

Study to show thyself approved unto God, a workman that needeth not to be ashamed, rightly dividing the word of truth. (2 Timothy 2:15)

God's Truth Is Our Shield and Our Buckler

He shall cover thee with his feathers, and under his wings shalt thou trust: his truth shall be thy shield and buckler. (Psalm 91:4)

God's Truth Preserves Us

Withhold not thou thy tender mercies from me, O LORD: let thy lovingkindness and thy truth continually preserve me. (Psalm 40:11)

God's Truth Enables Us to Stand

Wherefore take unto you the whole armour of God, that ye may be able to withstand in the evil day, and having done all, to stand. Stand therefore, having your loins girt about with truth. (Ephesians 6:13-14)

We Are to Walk in the Truth

I have no greater joy than to hear that my children walk in truth. (3 John 1:4)

We Are to Rejoice in the Truth

Rejoiceth not in iniquity, but rejoiceth in the truth. (1 Corinthians 13:6)

We Are to Be Men and Women of Truth

Moreover thou shalt provide out of all the people able men, such as fear God, men of truth. (Exodus 18:21)

We Are to Be Fellowhelpers to the Truth

We therefore ought to receive such, that we might be fellowhelpers to the truth. (3 John 1:8)

We Are to Be Thankful for Those Who Believe the Truth

But we are bound to give thanks alway to God for you, brethren beloved of the Lord, because God hath from the beginning chosen you to salvation through sanctification of the Spirit and belief of the truth. (2 Thessalonians 2:13)

God Will Judge the World With His Righteousness and Truth

Before the LORD: for he cometh, for he cometh to judge the earth: he shall judge the world with righteousness, and the people with his truth. (Psalm 96:13)

God's Truth Reaches up to the Clouds

For thy mercy is great above the heavens: and thy truth reacheth unto the clouds. (Psalm 108:4)

God's Truth Endureth Forever

O Praise the LORD, all ye nations: praise him, all ye people. For his merciful kindness is great toward us: and the truth of the LORD endureth for ever. (Psalm 117:1-2)

Hope Is Laid up in Heaven From Hearing the Truth of the Gospel

For the hope which is laid up for you in heaven, whereof ye heard before in the word of the truth of the gospel; Which is come unto you, as it is in all the world; and bringeth forth fruit, as it doth also in you, since the day ye heard of it, and knew the grace of God in truth. (Colossians 1:5-6)

He Who Does Truth Comes to the Light

But he that doeth truth cometh to the light, that his deeds may be made manifest, that they are wrought in God. (John 3:21)

But There Are Those Who Are Not Valiant for the Truth

And they bend their tongues like their bow for lies: but they are not valiant for the truth upon the earth; for they proceed from evil to evil, and they know not me, saith the Lord. (Jeremiah 9:3)

Some Do Not Have a Love of the Truth

Even him, whose coming is after the working of Satan with all power and signs and lying wonders, And with all deceivableness of unrighteousness in them that perish; because they received not the love of the truth, that they might be saved. (2 Thessalonians 2:9-10)

Some Do Not Believe the Truth

And for this cause God shall send them strong delusion, that they should believe a lie: That they all might be damned who believed not the truth, but had pleasure in unrighteousness. (2 Thessalonians 2:11-12)

Some Call on God but Not in Truth

Hear ye this, O house of Jacob, which are called by the name of Israel, and are come forth out of the waters of Judah, which swear by the name of the Lord, and make mention of the God of Israel, but not in truth, nor in righteousness. (Isaiah 48:1)

There Are People Who Turn Away From the Truth

For the time will come when they will not endure sound doctrine; but after their own lusts shall they heap to themselves teachers, having itching ears; And they shall turn away their ears from the truth, and shall be turned unto fables. (2 Timothy 4:3-4)

We Are to Warn Those Who Err From the Truth

Brethren, if any of you do err from the truth, and one convert him; Let him know, that he which converteth the sinner from the error of his way shall save a soul from death, and shall hide a multitude of sins. (James 5:19-20)

Some Change the Truth of God Into a Lie

Who changed the truth of God into a lie, and worshipped and served the creature more than the Creator, who is blessed for ever. (Romans 1:25)

Speak the Truth With Your Neighbor

Wherefore putting away lying, speak every man truth with his neighbour: for we are members one of another. (Ephesians 4:25)

No Lie Is of the Truth

I have not written unto you because ye know not the truth, but because ye know it, and that no lie is of the truth. (1 John 2:21)

The Devil Has No Truth in Him

He was a murderer from the beginning, and abode not in the truth, because there is no truth in him. When he speaketh a lie, he speaketh of his own: for he is a liar, and the father of it. (John 8:44)

The Truth Shall Be Spoken of as Evil

But there were false prophets also among the people, even as there shall be false teachers among you, who privily shall bring in damnable heresies, even denying the Lord that bought them, and bring upon themselves swift destruction. And many shall follow their pernicious ways; by reason of whom the way of truth shall be evil spoken of. (2 Peter 2:1-2)

Truth Is Largely Fallen

And judgment is turned away backward, and justice standeth afar off: for truth is fallen in the street, and equity cannot enter. (Isaiah 59:14)

Choose Truth

I have chosen the way of truth: thy judgments have I laid before me. (Psalm 119:30)

The Truth Shall Make You Free

Then said Jesus to those Jews which believed on him, If ye continue in my word, then are ye my disciples indeed; And ye shall know the truth, and the truth shall make you free. (John 8:31-32)

TRUTH OR CONSEQUENCES

TRUTH OR CONSEQUENCES. The stakes are high, but one thing is for sure: Truth prevails in the end because Jesus Christ is the way, *the truth*, and the life (John 14:6) and His *truth* endures forever (Psalm 117:1-2). May we pray that His *truth* will shine forth in our lives and that many will be turned to righteousness (Matthew 5:16, Daniel 12:3). And when it is all said and done, let us be able to say that we have "chosen the way of truth" (Psalm 119:30), that we have "walked" in God's truth (Psalm 26:3), and that we have always "rejoiced" in God's truth (1 Corinthians 13:6).

Pray for the Truth

O send out thy light and thy truth: let them lead me. (Psalm 43:3)

Teach me thy way, O Lord; I will walk in thy truth. (Psalm 86:11)

Show me thy ways, O Lord; teach me thy paths. Lead me in thy truth, and teach me: for thou art the God of my salvation; on thee do I wait all the day. (Psalm 25:4-5)

God Is Our Refuge and Our Strength

God is our refuge and our strength,
Our ever present aid,
And, therefore, though the Earth gives way,
We will not be afraid;
Though hills amidst the sea be cast,
Though foaming waters roar,
Yea, though the mighty billows shake
The mountains on the shore.

O come, behold what wondrous works
The Lord's great might has wrought;
Come, see what desolation great
He on the Earth has brought.
To utmost ends of all the earth
He causes war to cease;
The weapons of the strong destroyed,
He makes abiding peace.

Be still and know that I am God,
O'er all exalted high;
The subject nations of the Earth
My name shall magnify.
The Lord of hosts is on our side,
Our safety to secure;
The God of Jacob is for us
A refuge strong and sure.

Arthur Sullivan (1867)

5

GOD'S STRENGTH

God is our refuge and strength, a very present help in trouble. (Psalm 46:1)

Throughout the Bible, we are told to rely on God's strength and not our own. And throughout life—especially in times of trouble—the Bible makes it clear that God is our refuge and strength (Psalm 46:1).

God tells the apostle Paul that His grace is sufficient in all circumstances because He will provide His strength in our weakness (2 Corinthians 12:9). And with obvious irony, Paul makes the point that even *if* God had any weakness—which He doesn't—that weakness would be stronger than the strongest strength of men (1 Corinthians 1:25).

The bottom line is that to get through this life in a manner that is pleasing and glorifying to God, we need to solely rely on God's powerful and perfect strength. It's in that strength that we will be able to stand, even in the darkest days. In Edith G. Cherry 1895 hymn, "We Rest on Thee, Our Shield and Our Defender!" She writes:

We go not forth alone against the foe;
Strong in thy strength, safe in thy keeping tender,
We rest on thee, and in thy name we go.

Many of us first heard about God's strength in the lyrics of the children's song "Jesus Loves Me." It was written in 1860 by Anna B. Warner:

Jesus loves me! This I know,
For the Bible tells me so;
Little ones to Him belong,
They are weak, but He is strong.

BE STRONG IN THE LORD

THE APOSTLE PAUL exhorted the Ephesians to be strong in the Lord and in the power of His might so they could stand against the wiles of the Devil.

> Finally, my brethren, be strong in the Lord, and in the power of his might. Put on the whole armour of God, that ye may be able to stand against the wiles of the devil. (Ephesians 6:10-11)

NOT OUR OWN STRENGTH

WE ARE OFTEN reminded that our own strength is futile in the ongoing spiritual battle. We need God's strength—it is He who wins the battle. God tells the apostle Paul:

> My grace is sufficient for thee: for my strength is made perfect in weakness. Most gladly therefore will I rather glory in my infirmities, that the power of Christ may rest upon me. Therefore I take pleasure in infirmities, in reproaches, in necessities, in persecutions, in distresses for Christ's sake: for when I am weak, then am I strong. (2 Corinthians 12:9-10)

GOD OUR STRENGTH

GOD'S STRENGTH IS also the main theme of Fanny Crosby's 1882 hymn, *God Our Strength, Enthroned Above*:

God of our strength, enthroned above,
The source of life, the fount of love,
O let devotion's sacred flame
Our souls awake to praise thy name.
God of our strength, we wait on thee,
Our sure defense forever be.

The fact that His strength is available to us is echoed throughout the Bible. The following Scriptures declare the grace and power of our strong and mighty God and our continual need for His victorious strength in our daily lives. May we let these Scriptures change us so that we truly walk in the strength of the Lord.

THE LORD'S STRENGTH

The Lord Is Strong

O Lord God of hosts, who is a strong Lord like unto thee? (Psalm 89:8)

Who is this King of glory? The Lord strong and mighty, the Lord mighty in battle. (Psalm 24:8)

Their Redeemer is strong; the Lord of hosts is his name. (Jeremiah 50:34)

The Lord Is Our Strong Refuge

I am as a wonder unto many; but thou art my strong refuge. (Psalm 71:7)

The Lord Is Our Strong Tower

For thou hast been a shelter for me, and a strong tower from the enemy. (Psalm 61:3)

The Lord Is Our Strong Rock

Bow down thine ear to me; deliver me speedily: be thou my strong rock, for an house of defence to save me. (Psalm 31:2)

The Lord's Strength

Ascribe ye strength unto God: his excellency is over Israel, and his strength is in the clouds. (Psalm 68:34)

Be thou exalted, Lord, in thine own strength: so will we sing and praise thy power. (Psalm 21:13)

The Lord Is Clothed With Strength

The Lord reigneth, he is clothed with majesty; the Lord is clothed with strength, wherewith he hath girded himself: the world also is stablished, that it cannot be moved. (Psalm 93:1)

God Declares His Strength

Thou art the God that doest wonders: thou hast declared thy strength among the people. (Psalm 77:14)

We Declare His Strength

I will open my mouth in a parable: I will utter dark sayings of old: Which we have heard and known, and our fathers have told us. We will not hide them from their children, shewing to the generation to come the praises of the LORD, and his strength, and his wonderful works that he hath done. (Psalm 78:2-4)

Strength and Gladness Reside With the Lord

Glory and honour are in his presence; strength and gladness are in his place. (1 Chronicles 16:27)

Show God's Strength When You Are Old

Now also when I am old and greyheaded, O God, forsake me not; until I have showed thy strength unto this generation, and thy power to every one that is to come. (Psalm 71:18)

THE LORD OUR STRENGTH

The Lord Is Our Strength

I will love thee, O Lord, my strength. (Psalm 18:1)

The Lord Is Our Strength and Our Power

God is my strength and power: And he maketh my way perfect. He maketh my feet like hinds' feet: and setteth me upon my high places. (2 Samuel 22:33-34)

The Lord Is Our Strength and Our Light

The Lord is my light and my salvation; whom shall I fear? the Lord is the strength of my life; of whom shall I be afraid? (Psalm 27:1)

The Lord Is Our Strength and Defense

Unto thee, O my strength, will I sing: for God is my defence, and the God of my mercy. (Psalm 59:17)

The Lord Is Our Strength and Our Refuge

In God is my salvation and my glory: the rock of my strength, and my refuge, is in God. (Psalm 62:7)

The Lord Is Our Strength and Our Fortress

O Lord, my strength, and my fortress, and my refuge in the day of affliction. (Jeremiah 16:19)

The Lord Is Our Strength and Our Shield

The Lord is my strength and my shield; my heart trusted in him, and I am helped: therefore my heart greatly rejoiceth. (Psalm 28:7)

The Lord Is Our Strength and Our Rock

The Lord is my rock, and my fortress, and my deliverer; my God, my strength, in whom I will trust; my buckler, and the horn of my salvation, and my high tower. (Psalm 18:2)

The Lord Is Our Strength and Our Song

The Lord is my strength and song, and is become my salvation. (Psalm 118:14)

Behold, God is my salvation; I will trust, and not be afraid: for the Lord Jehovah is my strength and my song; he also is become my salvation. (Isaiah 12:2)

God Is the Strength of Our Heart

My flesh and my heart faileth: but God is the strength of my heart, and my portion for ever. (Psalm 73:26)

God Is Strength to the Upright

The way of the Lord is strength to the upright: but destruction shall be to the workers of iniquity. (Proverbs 10:29)

God Is the Strength of Our Salvation

O God the Lord, the strength of my salvation, thou hast covered my head in the day of battle. (Psalm 140:7)

The Lord Is Our Saving Strength

The Lord is their strength, and he is the saving strength of his anointed. (Psalm 28:8)

The Lord Is Our Everlasting Strength

Trust ye in the Lord for ever: for in the LORD JEHOVAH is everlasting strength. (Isaiah 26:4)

Blessed Are Those Whose Strength Is in God

Blessed is the man whose strength is in thee; in whose heart are the ways of them. (Psalm 84:5)

He Guides Us With His Strength

Thou in thy mercy hast led forth the people which thou hast redeemed: thou hast guided them in thy strength unto thy holy habitation. (Exodus 15:13)

God's Strength in the Mouths of Babes

Out of the mouth of babes and sucklings hast thou ordained strength because of thine enemies, that thou mightest still the enemy and the avenger. (Psalm 8:2)

God Saves With the Strength of His Right Hand

Now know I that the LORD saveth his anointed; he will hear him from his holy heaven with the saving strength of his right hand. (Psalm 20:6)

BE STRONG IN THE LORD

Be Strong in the Lord

Be strong, and quit yourselves like men. (1 Samuel 4:9)

Be Strong in the Power of the Lord's Might

Finally, my brethren, be strong in the Lord, and in the power of his might. Put on the whole armour of God, that ye may be able to stand against the wiles of the devil. (Ephesians 6:10-11)

Be Strong and of Good Courage

Be strong and of a good courage, fear not, nor be afraid of them: for the LORD thy God, he it is that doth go with thee; he will not fail thee, nor forsake thee. (Deuteronomy 31:6)

Be Strong in God's Grace

Thou therefore, my son, be strong in the grace that is in Christ Jesus. (2 Timothy 2:1)

Be Strong, and Do Exploits

And such as do wickedly against the covenant shall he corrupt by flatteries: but the people that do know their God shall be strong, and do exploits. (Daniel 11:32)

GOD WILL STRENGTHEN US

The Lord Gives Us Strength

The LORD will give strength unto his people; the LORD will bless his people with peace. (Psalm 29:11)

Fear thou not; for I am with thee: be not dismayed; for I am thy God: I will strengthen thee; yea, I will help thee; yea, I will uphold thee with the right hand of my righteousness. (Isaiah 41:10)

Wait on the Lord, and He Will Strengthen Us

Wait on the LORD: be of good courage, and he shall strengthen thine heart: wait, I say, on the LORD. (Psalm 27:14)

But they that wait upon the LORD shall renew their strength; they shall mount up with wings as eagles; they shall run, and not be weary; and they shall walk, and not faint. (Isaiah 40:31)

God Will Strengthen Our Heart

Be of good courage, and he shall strengthen your heart, all ye that hope in the LORD. (Psalm 31:24)

God Will Give Us Strength and Power

O God, thou art terrible out of thy holy places: the God of Israel is he that giveth strength and power unto his people. Blessed be God. (Psalm 68:35)

God Girds Us With His Strength

It is God that girdeth me with strength, and maketh my way perfect. (Psalm 18:32)

God Gives Strength to Them With No Might

He giveth power to the faint; and to them that have no might he increaseth strength. (Isaiah 40:29)

God Strengthens Us in Our Soul

In the day when I cried thou answeredst me, and strengthenedst me with strength in my soul. (Psalm 138:3)

Jesus Christ Can Strengthen Us in All Things

I can do all things through Christ which strengtheneth me. (Philippians 4:13)

Go in the Strength of the Lord

I will go in the strength of the Lord GOD. (Psalm 71:16)

THE LORD'S STRENGTH DEMONSTRATED

The Lord's Strength in Sara

Through faith also Sara herself received strength to conceive seed, and was delivered of a child when she was past age, because she judged him faithful who had promised. (Hebrews 11:11)

The Lord's Strength in the Israelites

And it shall be when thy son asketh thee in time to come, saying, What is this? that thou shalt say unto him, By strength of hand the LORD brought us out from Egypt, from the house of bondage. (Exodus 13:14)

The Lord's Strength in Joshua

And Joshua said unto them, Fear not, nor be dismayed, be strong and of good courage: for thus shall the LORD do to all your enemies against whom ye fight. (Joshua 10:25)

The Lord's Strength in Samson

And Samson called unto the LORD, and said, O Lord GOD, remember me, I pray thee, and strengthen me, I pray thee, only this once, O God, that I may be at once avenged of the Philistines for my two eyes. (Judges 16:28)

The Lord's Strength in Ezra

And hath extended mercy unto me before the king, and his counsellors, and before all the king's mighty princes. And I was strengthened as the hand of the LORD my God was upon me, and I gathered together out of Israel chief men to go up with me. (Ezra 7:28)

The Lord's Strength in David

A Psalm of David, the servant of the LORD, who spake unto the LORD the words of this song in the day that the LORD delivered him from the hand of all his enemies, and from the hand of Saul: And he said, I will love thee, O LORD, my strength. (Psalm 18:1)

The Lord's Strength in Isaiah

And now, saith the LORD that formed me from the womb to be his servant, to bring Jacob again to him, Though Israel be not gathered, yet shall I be glorious in the eyes of the LORD, and my God shall be my strength. (Isaiah 49:5)

The Lord's Strength in Jeremiah

O LORD, my strength, and my fortress, and my refuge in the day of affliction. (Jeremiah 16:19)

The Lord's Strength in Ezekiel

So the spirit lifted me up, and took me away, and I went in bitterness, in the heat of my spirit; but the hand of the LORD was strong upon me. (Ezekiel 3:14)

The Lord's Strength in Daniel

And said, O man greatly beloved, fear not: peace be unto thee, be strong, yea, be strong. And when he had spoken unto me, I was strengthened, and said, Let my lord speak; for thou hast strengthened me. (Daniel 10:19)

The Lord's Strength in Paul

Notwithstanding the Lord stood with me, and strengthened me; that by me the preaching might be fully known, and that all the Gentiles might hear: and I was delivered out of the mouth of the lion. (2 Timothy 4:17)

The Lord's Strength in Others

And what shall I more say? for the time would fail me to tell of Gideon, and of Barak, and of Samson, and of

Jephthae; of David also, and Samuel, and of the prophets: Who through faith subdued kingdoms, wrought righteousness, obtained promises, stopped the mouths of lions, Quenched the violence of fire, escaped the edge of the sword, out of weakness were made strong, waxed valiant in fight, turned to flight the armies of the aliens. (Hebrews 11:32-34)

GOD'S STRENGTH IN TIMES OF TROUBLE

God Is Our Strength in Times of Trouble

God is our refuge and strength, a very present help in trouble. Therefore will not we fear, though the earth be removed, and though the mountains be carried into the midst of the sea. (Psalm 46:1-2)

But the salvation of the righteous is of the Lord: he is their strength in the time of trouble. (Psalm 37:39)

God Is Strength to the Needy in Distress

For thou hast been a strength to the poor, a strength to the needy in his distress, a refuge from the storm, a shadow from the heat, when the blast of the terrible ones is as a storm against the wall. (Isaiah 25:4)

God Girds Us With Strength for the Battle

For thou hast girded me with strength unto the battle: thou hast subdued under me those that rose up against me. (Psalm 18:39)

MAN'S STRENGTH IS FUTILE

Man's Strength Will Not Prevail

He will keep the feet of his saints, and the wicked shall be silent in darkness; for by strength shall no man prevail. (1 Samuel 2:9)

Man Not Making God His Strength

Lo, this is the man that made not God his strength; but trusted in the abundance of his riches, and strengthened himself in his wickedness. (Psalm 52:7)

Forgetting God and His Strength

Because thou hast forgotten the God of thy salvation, and hast not been mindful of the rock of thy strength, therefore shalt thou plant pleasant plants, and shalt set it with strange slips. (Isaiah 17:10)

Not by Men's Might nor by Men's Power

Not by might, nor by power, but by my spirit, saith the LORD of hosts. (Zechariah 4:6)

PRAYERS FOR GOD'S STRENGTH

Be Not Far From Me

But be not thou far from me, O LORD: O my strength, haste thee to help me. (Psalm 22:19)

Pull Me Out of the Adversaries Net

Pull me out of the net that they have laid privily for me: for thou art my strength. (Psalm 31:4)

Strengthen My Hands

For they all made us afraid, saying, Their hands shall be weakened from the work, that it be not done. Now therefore, O God, strengthen my hands. (Nehemiah 6:9)

Strengthen Me With Thy Might

For this cause I bow my knees unto the Father of our Lord Jesus Christ, Of whom the whole family in heaven and earth is named, That he would grant you, according to the riches of his glory, to be strengthened with might by his Spirit in the inner man. (Ephesians 3:14-16)

For this cause we also, since the day we heard it, do not cease to pray for you, and to desire that ye might be filled with the knowledge of his will in all wisdom and spiritual understanding; That ye might walk worthy of the Lord unto all pleasing, being fruitful in every good work, and increasing in the knowledge of God; Strengthened with all might, according to his glorious power, unto all patience and longsuffering with joyfulness. (Colossians 1:9-11)

Be My Strong Habitation

Be thou my strong habitation, whereunto I may continually resort: thou hast given commandment to save me; for thou art my rock and my fortress. (Psalm 71:3)

Strengthen Me, Settle Me

But the God of all grace, who hath called us unto his eternal glory by Christ Jesus, after that ye have suffered a while, make you perfect, stablish, strengthen, settle you. (1 Peter 5:10)

Strengthen Me According to Thy Word

My soul melteth for heaviness: strengthen thou me according unto thy word. (Psalm 119:28)

Strengthen the Things That Remain

[S]trengthen the things that remain. (Revelation 3:2)

Be My Strong Rock

Bow down thine ear to me; deliver me speedily: be thou my strong rock, for an house of defence to save me. (Psalm 31:2)

Give Me Thy Strength

O turn unto me, and have mercy upon me; give thy strength unto thy servant. (Psalm 86:16)

Strengthen Me in My Old Age

Cast me not off in the time of old age; forsake me not when my strength faileth. (Psalm 71:9)

BENEDICTION

Let the words of my mouth, and the meditation of my heart, be acceptable in thy sight, O Lord, my strength, and my redeemer. (Psalm 19:14)

6

GROWING SPIRITUALLY

> But grow in grace, and in the knowledge of our Lord and Saviour Jesus Christ. To him be glory both now and for ever. (2 Peter 3:18)

GOD OVERSEES OUR GROWTH

David wanted to grow and mature in the Lord. In Psalm 51, he seeks and cries out to God to create a clean heart within him. In Psalm 139, David further seeks God, asking Him to search his heart, to try him and to know his thoughts, to see if there is anything hidden there—and to lead him in the way everlasting (Psalm 139:23-24). And the prophet Isaiah makes it clear that God oversees and shapes our personal and spiritual growth. The Lord is the "potter" and we are the "clay" and the work of His hand.

> But now, O LORD, thou art our father; we are the clay, and thou our potter; and we all are the work of thy hand. (Isaiah 64:8)

The apostle Paul affirms that we are the work of God's hand in the New Testament when he describes believers as God's "workmanship" (Ephesians 2:10). He perfects and purifies those who have faith that He *can* and *will* make us whole. As believers, we come to understand that everything we need to know for our spiritual well-being is fully described in the pages of the Bible. We also find that many of the prayers in Scripture can be directly applied for our own personal and spiritual growth.

Pray and Grow

Hear my prayer, O Lord, and give ear unto my cry. (Psalm 39:12)

100 SHORT SCRIPTURAL PRAYERS

Anchor Me

Which hope [in God] we have as an anchor of the soul, both sure and stedfast, and which entereth into that within the veil. (Hebrews 6:19)

Anoint Me

Thou preparest a table before me in the presence of mine enemies: thou anointest my head with oil; My cup runneth over. (Psalm 23:5)

Answer Me

Hear, O Lord, when I cry with my voice: have mercy also upon me, and answer me. (Psalm 27:7)

Awaken Me

And that, knowing the time, that now it is high time to awake out of sleep: for now is our salvation nearer than when we believed. (Romans 13:11)

Bind Me

I will seek that which was lost, and bring again that which was driven away, and will bind up that which was broken. (Ezekiel 34:16)

Calm Me

Thou wilt keep him in perfect peace, whose mind is stayed on thee: because he trusteth in thee. (Isaiah 26:3)

Carry Me

And even to your old age I am he; and even to hoar hairs will I carry you: I have made, and I will bear; even I will carry, and will deliver you. (Isaiah 46:4)

Cleanse Me

Who can understand his errors? cleanse thou me from secret faults. (Psalm 19:12)

Comfort Me

Blessed be God, even the Father of our Lord Jesus Christ, the Father of mercies, and the God of all comfort; Who comforteth us in all our tribulation, that we may be able to comfort them which are in any trouble, by the comfort wherewith we ourselves are comforted of God. (2 Corinthians 1:3-4)

Complete Me

Being confident of this very thing, that he which hath begun a good work in you will perform it until the day of Jesus Christ. (Philippians 1:6)

Confirm Me

Who shall also confirm you unto the end, that ye may be blameless in the day of our Lord Jesus Christ. (1 Corinthians 1:8)

Conform Me

For whom he did foreknow, he also did predestinate to be conformed to the image of his Son, that he might be the firstborn among many brethren. (Romans 8:29)

Console Me

Now our Lord Jesus Christ himself, and God, even our Father, which hath loved us, and hath given us everlasting consolation and good hope through grace, Comfort your hearts, and stablish you in every good word and work. (2 Thessalonians 2:16-17)

Correct Me

O Lord, correct me, but with judgment; not in thine anger, lest thou bring me to nothing. (Jeremiah 10:24)

Counsel Me

Thou shalt guide me with thy counsel, and afterward receive me to glory. (Psalm 73:24)

Cover Me

He shall cover thee with his feathers, and under his wings shalt thou trust: his truth shall be thy shield and buckler. (Psalm 91:4)

Defend Me

O my God: defend me from them that rise up against me. (Psalm 59:1)

Deliver Me

O Lord my God, in thee do I put my trust: save me from all them that persecute me, and deliver me. (Psalm 7:1)

Direct Me

In all thy ways acknowledge him, and he shall direct thy paths. (Proverbs 3:6)

Draw Me

And I, if I be lifted up from the earth, will draw all men unto me. (John 12:32)

Embolden Me

Herein is our love made perfect, that we may have boldness in the day of judgment: because as he is, so are we in this world. (1 John 4:17)

Empower Me

He giveth power to the faint; and to them that have no might he increaseth strength. (Isaiah 40:29)

Enable Me

And I thank Christ Jesus our Lord, who hath enabled me. (1 Timothy 1:12)

Enlarge Me

Hear me when I call, O God of my righteousness: thou hast enlarged me when I was in distress; have mercy upon me, and hear my prayer. (Psalm 4:1)

Enlighten Me

For thou wilt light my candle: the LORD my God will enlighten my darkness. (Psalm 18:28)

Enrich Me

That in every thing ye are enriched by him, in all utterance, and in all knowledge. (1 Corinthians 1:5)

Examine Me

Examine me, O LORD, and prove me; try my reins and my heart. (Psalm 26:2)

Feed Me

He shall feed his flock like a shepherd: he shall gather the lambs with his arm, and carry them in his bosom, and shall gently lead those that are with young. (Isaiah 40:11)

Fill Me

That Christ may dwell in your hearts by faith; that ye, being rooted and grounded in love, May be able to comprehend with all saints what is the breadth, and length, and depth, and height; And to know the love of Christ, which passeth knowledge, that ye might be filled with all the fulness of God. (Ephesians 3:17-19)

Forgive Me

For thou, Lord, art good, and ready to forgive; and plenteous in mercy unto all them that call upon thee. (Psalm 86:5)

Form Me

My little children, of whom I travail in birth again until Christ be formed in you. (Galatians 4:19)

Free Me

If the Son therefore shall make you free, ye shall be free indeed. (John 8:36)

Gather Me

Save us, O Lord our God, and gather us from among the heathen, to give thanks unto thy holy name, and to triumph in thy praise. (Psalm 106:47)

Gird Me

It is God that girdeth me with strength, and maketh my way perfect. He maketh my feet like hinds' feet, and setteth me upon my high places. (Psalm 18:32-33)

Ground Me

That he would grant you, according to the riches of his glory, to be strengthened with might by his Spirit in the inner man; That Christ may dwell in your hearts by faith; that ye, being rooted and grounded in love. (Ephesians 3:16-17)

Grow Me

But unto you that fear my name shall the Sun of righteousness arise with healing in his wings; and ye shall go forth, and grow up as calves of the stall. (Malachi 4:2)

Guide Me

For thou art my rock and my fortress; therefore for thy name's sake lead me, and guide me. (Psalm 31:3)

Heal Me

Heal me, O Lord, and I shall be healed. (Jeremiah 17:14)

Hear Me

Hear me, O Lord; for thy lovingkindness is good: turn unto me according to the multitude of thy tender mercies. (Psalm 69:16)

Help Me

Help me, O Lord my God: O save me according to thy mercy. (Psalm 109:26)

Hide Me

Hide me from the secret counsel of the wicked; from the insurrection of the workers of iniquity. (Psalm 64:2)

Hold Me

Even there shall thy hand lead me, and thy right hand shall hold me. (Psalm 139:10)

Increase Me

So then neither is he that planteth any thing, neither he that watereth; but God that giveth the increase. (1 Corinthians 3:7)

Inspire Me

But there is a spirit in man: and the inspiration of the Almighty giveth them understanding. (Job 32:8)

Instruct Me

I will instruct thee and teach thee in the way which thou shalt go. (Psalm 32:8)

Judge Me

Judge me, O Lord my God, according to thy righteousness; and let them not rejoice over me. (Psalm 35:24)

Keep Me

Keep me as the apple of the eye, hide me under the shadow of thy wings, From the wicked that oppress me, from my deadly enemies, who compass me about. (Psalm 17:8-9)

Know Me

Search me, O God, and know my heart: try me, and know my thoughts. (Psalm 139:23)

Lead Me

Lead me in thy truth, and teach me: for thou art the God of my salvation; on thee do I wait all the day. (Psalm 25:5)

Lift Me

Humble yourselves in the sight of the Lord, and he shall lift you up. (James 4:10)

Love Me

He that hath my commandments, and keepeth them, he it is that loveth me: and he that loveth me shall be loved of my Father, and I will love him, and will manifest myself to him. (John 14:21)

Perfect Me

The LORD will perfect that which concerneth me. (Psalm 138:8)

Polish Me

And he hath made my mouth like a sharp sword; in the shadow of his hand hath he hid me, and made me a polished shaft. (Isaiah 49:2)

Prepare Me

LORD, thou hast heard the desire of the humble: thou wilt prepare their heart. (Psalm 10:17)

Preserve Me

Preserve me, O God: for in thee do I put my trust. (Psalm 16:1)

Protect Me

But let all those that put their trust in thee rejoice: let them ever shout for joy, because thou defendest them: let them also that love thy name be joyful in thee. (Psalm 5:11)

Prove Me

Examine me, O Lord, and prove me; try my reins and my heart. (Psalm 26:2)

Purge Me

Help us, O God of our salvation, for the glory of thy name: and deliver us, and purge away our sins, for thy name's sake. (Psalm 79:9)

Purify Me

Looking for that blessed hope, and the glorious appearing of the great God and our Saviour Jesus Christ; Who gave himself for us, that he might redeem us from all iniquity, and purify unto himself a peculiar people, zealous of good works. (Titus 2:13-14)

Quench Me

In the last day, that great day of the feast, Jesus stood and cried, saying, If any man thirst, let him come unto me, and drink. (John 7:37)

Quicken Me

Quicken me, O Lord, for thy name's sake: for thy righteousness' sake bring my soul out of trouble. (Psalm 143:11)

Quiet Me

But whoso hearkeneth unto me shall dwell safely, and shall be quiet from fear of evil. (Proverbs 1:33)

Raise Me

The Lord upholdeth all that fall, and raiseth up all those that be bowed down. (Psalm 145:14)

Receive Me

But God will redeem my soul from the power of the grave: for he shall receive me. (Psalm 49:15)

Recover Me

O Lord, by these things men live, and in all these things is the life of my spirit: so wilt thou recover me, and make me to live. (Isaiah 38:16)

Redeem Me

But as for me, I will walk in mine integrity: redeem me, and be merciful unto me. (Psalm 26:11)

Refine Me

Behold, I have refined thee, but not with silver; I have chosen thee in the furnace of affliction. (Isaiah 48:10)

Remember Me

Remember me, O Lord, with the favour that thou bearest unto thy people. (Psalm 106:4)

Renew Me

Create in me a clean heart, O God; and renew a right spirit within me. (Psalm 51:10)

Replenish Me

For I have satiated the weary soul, and I have replenished every sorrowful soul. (Jeremiah 31:25)

Rescue Me

Lord, how long wilt thou look on? rescue my soul from their destructions, my darling from the lions. (Psalm 35:17)

Restore Me

Restore unto me the joy of thy salvation; and uphold me with thy free spirit. (Psalm 51:12)

Revive Me

Though I walk in the midst of trouble, thou wilt revive me. (Psalm 138:7)

Sanctify Me

And the very God of peace sanctify you wholly; and I pray God your whole spirit and soul and body be preserved blameless unto the coming of our Lord Jesus Christ. (1 Thessalonians 5:23)

Satisfy Me

For he satisfieth the longing soul, and filleth the hungry soul with goodness. (Psalm 107:9)

Save Me

Save me, O God; for the waters are come in unto my soul. (Psalm 69:1)

Search Me

Search me, O God, and know my heart: try me, and know my thoughts: And see if there be any wicked way in me, and lead me in the way everlasting. (Psalm 139:23-24)

Seek Me

I have gone astray like a lost sheep; seek thy servant; for I do not forget thy commandments. (Psalm 119:176)

Send Me

Also I heard the voice of the Lord, saying, Whom shall I send, and who will go for us? Then said I, Here am I; send me. (Isaiah 6:8)

Settle Me

But the God of all grace, who hath called us unto his eternal glory by Christ Jesus, after that ye have suffered a while, make you perfect, stablish, strengthen, settle you. (1 Peter 5:10)

Shelter Me

For thou hast been a shelter for me, and a strong tower from the enemy. (Psalm 61:3)

Shepherd Me

The LORD is my shepherd; I shall not want. (Psalm 23:1)

Shield Me

But thou, O LORD, art a shield for me; my glory, and the lifter up of mine head. (Psalm 3:3)

Show Me

Shew me thy ways, O LORD; teach me thy paths. (Psalm 25:4)

Spare Me

O spare me, that I may recover strength, before I go hence, and be no more. (Psalm 39:13)

Stablish Me

But the Lord is faithful, who shall stablish you, and keep you from evil. (2 Thessalonians 3:3)

Strengthen Me

My soul melteth for heaviness: strengthen thou me according unto thy word. (Psalm 119:28)

Supply Me

But my God shall supply all your need according to his riches in glory by Christ Jesus. (Philippians 4:19)

Sustain Me

Cast thy burden upon the LORD, and he shall sustain thee: he shall never suffer the righteous to be moved. (Psalm 55:22)

Teach Me

Teach me thy way, O LORD; I will walk in thy truth: unite my heart to fear thy name. (Psalm 86:11)

Touch Me

And Jesus came and touched them, and said, Arise, and be not afraid. (Matthew 17:7)

Transform Me

And be not conformed to this world: but be ye transformed by the renewing of your mind, that ye may prove what is that good, and acceptable, and perfect, will of God. (Romans 12:2)

Try Me

I the LORD search the heart, I try the reins, even to give every man according to his ways, and according to the fruit of his doings. (Jeremiah 17:10)

Turn Me

Turn us again, O God, and cause thy face to shine; and we shall be saved. (Psalm 80:3)

Use Me

But in a great house there are not only vessels of gold and of silver, but also of wood and of earth; and some to honour, and some to dishonour. If a man therefore purge himself from these, he shall be a vessel unto honour, sanctified, and meet for the master's use, and prepared unto every good work. (2 Timothy 2:20-21)

Uphold Me

Uphold me according unto thy word, that I may live: and let me not be ashamed of my hope. (Psalm 119:116)

Visit Me

O LORD, thou knowest: remember me, and visit me, and revenge me of my persecutors. (Jeremiah 15:15)

Wash Me

Wash me thoroughly from mine iniquity, and cleanse me from my sin. (Psalm 51:2)

Water Me

And the Lord shall guide thee continually, and satisfy thy soul in drought, and make fat thy bones: and thou shalt be like a watered garden, and like a spring of water, whose waters fail not. (Isaiah 58:11)

Wean Me

Whom shall he teach knowledge? and whom shall he make to understand doctrine? them that are weaned from the milk, and drawn from the breasts. (Isaiah 28:9)

MORE PRAYERS

As for me, I will call upon God; and the LORD shall save me. Evening, and morning, and at noon, will I pray, and cry aloud: and he shall hear my voice. (Psalm 55:16-17)

Have Mercy Upon Me—I am Weak

Have mercy upon me, O LORD; for I am weak: O LORD, heal me; for my bones are vexed. (Psalm 6:2)

Make Me Understand My Frailty

LORD, make me to know mine end, and the measure of my days, what it is; that I may know how frail I am. (Psalm 39:4)

Strengthen Me With Might in the Inner Man

For this cause I bow my knees unto the Father of our Lord Jesus Christ, Of whom the whole family in heaven and earth is named, That he would grant you, according to the riches of his glory, to be strengthened with might by his Spirit in the inner man. (Ephesians 3:14-16)

Let Me Search and Try My Ways

Let us search and try our ways, and turn again to the Lord. (Lamentations 3:40)

Make Me Know Truth in the Inner Parts

Behold, thou desirest truth in the inward parts: and in the hidden part thou shalt make me to know wisdom. (Psalm 51:6)

Help Me in My Unbelief

And straightway the father of the child cried out, and said with tears, Lord, I believe; help thou mine unbelief. (Mark 9:24)

Increase My Faith

And the apostles said unto the Lord, Increase our faith. (Luke 17:5)

Undertake For Me

O Lord, I am oppressed; undertake for me. (Isaiah 38:14)

Teach Me to Do Thy Will

Teach me to do thy will; for thou art my God: thy spirit is good; lead me into the land of uprightness. (Psalm 143:10)

Lead Me, O Lord

Lead me, O Lord, in thy righteousness because of mine enemies; make thy way straight before my face. (Psalm 5:8)

Order My Steps

Order my steps in thy word: and let not any iniquity have dominion over me. (Psalm 119:133)

Give Me Help From Trouble

Give us help from trouble: for vain is the help of man. (Psalm 60:11)

Let Me Not Be Ashamed

O my God, I trust in thee: let me not be ashamed, let not mine enemies triumph over me. (Psalm 25:2)

Deliver Me From My Fears

I sought the Lord, and he heard me, and delivered me from all my fears. (Psalm 34:4)

Keep Me From Snares

Keep me from the snares which they have laid for me, and the gins of the workers of iniquity. (Psalm 141:9)

Be My Hope in the Day of Evil

Be not a terror unto me: thou art my hope in the day of evil. (Jeremiah 17:17)

Keep My Soul

O keep my soul, and deliver me: let me not be ashamed; for I put my trust in thee. (Psalm 25:20)

Let Your Lovingkindness and Truth Preserve Me

Withhold not thou thy tender mercies from me, O Lord: let thy lovingkindness and thy truth continually preserve me. (Psalm 40:11)

Seek God and Grow

The Lord looked down from heaven upon the children of men, to see if there were any that did understand, and seek God. (Psalm 14:2)

Seek God and You Shall Find Him

. . . for the Lord searcheth all hearts, and understandeth all the imaginations of the thoughts: if thou seek him, he will be found of thee; but if thou forsake him, he will cast thee off for ever. (1 Chronicles 28:9)

Seek God While He May be Found

Seek ye the Lord while he may be found, call ye upon him while he is near. (Isaiah 55:6)

Seek God—Not a Sign

And he sighed deeply in his spirit, and saith, Why doth this generation seek after a sign? verily I say unto you, There shall no sign be given unto this generation. (Mark 8:12)

Seek God With All Your Heart

And ye shall seek me, and find me, when ye shall search for me with all your heart. (Jeremiah 29:13)

Seek God and Hearken Unto Him

Hearken to me, ye that follow after righteousness, ye that seek the LORD: look unto the rock whence ye are hewn, and to the hole of the pit whence ye are digged. (Isaiah 51:1)

Seek God and His Will

I can of mine own self do nothing: as I hear, I judge: and my judgment is just; because I seek not mine own will, but the will of the Father which hath sent me. (John 5:30)

Seek God and Rejoice

Let all those that seek thee rejoice and be glad in thee: and let such as love thy salvation say continually, Let God be magnified. (Psalm 70:4)

Seek God and You Will Not Be Forsaken

And they that know thy name will put their trust in thee: for thou, LORD, hast not forsaken them that seek thee. (Psalm 9:10)

Seek God and His Face Evermore

Seek the LORD, and his strength: seek his face evermore. (Psalm 105:4)

Seek God and to Dwell in His House

One thing have I desired of the LORD, that will I seek after; that I may dwell in the house of the LORD all the days of my life, to behold the beauty of the LORD, and to inquire in his temple. (Psalm 27:4)

Remember and Grow

When I remember these things, I pour out my soul in me. (Psalm 42:4)

God Is Our Helper

Behold, God is mine helper. (Psalm 54:4)

God Is Near to Those Who Call Upon Him

The Lord is nigh unto all them that call upon him, to all that call upon him in truth. (Psalm 145:18)

God Sent His Son

For God so loved the world, that he gave his only begotten Son, that whosoever believeth in him should not perish, but have everlasting life. (John 3:16)

We Are Saved by Confessing Jesus Christ

That if thou shalt confess with thy mouth the Lord Jesus, and shalt believe in thine heart that God hath raised him from the dead, thou shalt be saved. (Romans 10:9)

Jesus Christ Is Our Foundation

For other foundation can no man lay than that is laid, which is Jesus Christ. (1 Corinthians 3:11)

Jesus Christ Now Lives in Us

I am crucified with Christ: nevertheless I live; yet not I, but Christ liveth in me: and the life which I now live in the flesh I live by the faith of the Son of God, who loved me, and gave himself for me. (Galatians 2:20)

We Are a New Creation in Jesus Christ

Therefore if any man be in Christ, he is a new creature: old things are passed away; behold, all things are become new. (2 Corinthians 5:17)

Jesus Christ Is Being Formed in Us

My little children, of whom I travail in birth again until Christ be formed in you. (Galatians 4:19)

God Is the Potter, We Are the Clay

But now, O Lord, thou art our father; we are the clay, and thou our potter; and we all are the work of thy hand. (Isaiah 64:8)

We Are God's Workmanship

For we are his workmanship, created in Christ Jesus unto good works, which God hath before ordained that we should walk in them. (Ephesians 2:10)

The Holy Spirit Will Teach Us All Things

But the Comforter, which is the Holy Ghost, whom the Father will send in my name, he shall teach you all things, and bring all things to your remembrance, whatsoever I have said unto you. (John 14:26)

God Is For Us

What shall we then say to these things? If God be for us, who can be against us? (Romans 8:31)

God Is Our Guide

Thou shalt guide me with thy counsel, and afterward receive me to glory. (Psalm 73:24)

God Will Perfect His Work in Us

The LORD will perfect that which concerneth me. (Psalm 138:8)

God Will Never Leave Us or Forsake Us

Let your conversation be without covetousness; and be content with such things as ye have: for he hath said, I will never leave thee, nor forsake thee. (Hebrews 13:5)

Nothing Can Separate Us From the Love of God

For I am persuaded, that neither death, nor life, nor angels, nor principalities, nor powers, nor things present, nor things to come, Nor height, nor depth, nor any other creature, shall be able to separate us from the love of God, which is in Christ Jesus our Lord. (Romans 8:38-39)

God Is With Us Until the Very End

Teaching them to observe all things whatsoever I have commanded you: and, lo, I am with you alway, even unto the end of the world. (Matthew 28:20)

DO AND GROW

Those things, which ye have both learned, and received, and heard, and seen in me, do: and the God of peace shall be with you. (Philippians 4:9)

Set Your Affection on Things Above

If ye then be risen with Christ, seek those things which are above, where Christ sitteth on the right hand of God.

Set your affection on things above, not on things on the earth. (Colossians 3:1-2)

Call Unto God

Call unto me, and I will answer thee, and show thee great and mighty things, which thou knowest not. (Jeremiah 33:3)

Break Up Your Fallow Ground

Sow to yourselves in righteousness, reap in mercy; break up your fallow ground: for it is time to seek the Lord, till he come and rain righteousness upon you. (Hosea 10:12)

Draw Near to God

Draw nigh to God, and he will draw nigh to you. (James 4:8)

Pour Out Your Heart

Trust in him at all times; ye people, pour out your heart before him: God is a refuge for us. (Psalm 62:8)

Put Off the Old Man

That ye put off concerning the former conversation the old man, which is corrupt according to the deceitful lusts; And be renewed in the spirit of your mind; And that ye put on the new man, which after God is created in righteousness and true holiness. (Ephesians 4:22-24)

Purge Yourselves

Your glorying is not good. Know ye not that a little leaven leaveneth the whole lump? Purge out therefore the old leaven, that ye may be a new lump. (1 Corinthians 5:6-7)

Cleanse Yourselves

Having therefore these promises, dearly beloved, let us cleanse ourselves from all filthiness of the flesh and spirit, perfecting holiness in the fear of God. (2 Corinthians 7:1)

Cast off the Works of Darkness

The night is far spent, the day is at hand: let us therefore cast off the works of darkness, and let us put on the armour of light. (Romans 13:12)

Get the Log Out of Your Eye

Thou hypocrite, first cast out the beam out of thine own eye; and then shalt thou see clearly to cast out the mote out of thy brother's eye. (Matthew 7:5)

Cast Your Burden Upon the Lord

Cast thy burden upon the Lord, and he shall sustain thee: he shall never suffer the righteous to be moved. (Psalm 55:22)

Lean Not On Your Own Understanding

Trust in the Lord with all thine heart; and lean not unto thine own understanding. In all thy ways acknowledge him, and he shall direct thy paths. (Proverbs 3:5-6)

Ask God For Wisdom

If any of you lack wisdom, let him ask of God, that giveth to all men liberally, and upbraideth not; and it shall be given him. But let him ask in faith, nothing wavering. For he that wavereth is like a wave of the sea driven with the wind and tossed. (James 1:5-6)

Humble Yourselves

Humble yourselves therefore under the mighty hand of God, that he may exalt you in due time: Casting all your care upon him; for he careth for you. (1 Peter 5:6-7)

Examine Yourselves

Examine yourselves, whether ye be in the faith; prove your own selves. Know ye not your own selves, how that Jesus Christ is in you, except ye be reprobates? (2 Corinthians 13:5)

Judge Yourselves

For if we would judge ourselves, we should not be judged. (1 Corinthians 11:31)

Die to Self

For to me to live is Christ, and to die is gain. (Philippians 1:21)

Esteem Others Better Than Yourself

Let nothing be done through strife or vainglory; but in lowliness of mind let each esteem other better than themselves. (Philippians 2:3)

Forgive Others

For if ye forgive men their trespasses, your heavenly Father will also forgive you: But if ye forgive not men their trespasses, neither will your Father forgive your trespasses. (Matthew 6:14-15)

Love Your Enemy

Ye have heard that it hath been said, Thou shalt love thy neighbour, and hate thine enemy. But I say unto you, Love your enemies, bless them that curse you, do good to them that hate you, and pray for them which despitefully use you, and persecute you, (Matthew 5:43-44)

Put on the Whole Armour of God

Put on the whole armour of God, that ye may be able to stand against the wiles of the devil. (Ephesians 6:11)

Work Out Your Salvation With Fear and Trembling

Wherefore, my beloved, as ye have always obeyed, not as in my presence only, but now much more in my absence, work out your own salvation with fear and trembling. For it is God which worketh in you both to will and to do of his good pleasure. (Philippians 2:12-13)

Gird Up the Loins of Your Mind

Wherefore gird up the loins of your mind, be sober, and hope to the end for the grace that is to be brought unto you at the revelation of Jesus Christ. (1 Peter 1:13)

Take Every Thought Captive

Casting down imaginations, and every high thing that exalteth itself against the knowledge of God, and bringing into captivity every thought to the obedience of Christ. (2 Corinthians 10:5)

Please God Not Man

For do I now persuade men, or God? or do I seek to please men? for if I yet pleased men, I should not be the servant of Christ. (Galatians 1:10)

Study to Show Yourselves Approved

Study to show thyself approved unto God, a workman that needeth not to be ashamed, rightly dividing the word of truth. (2 Timothy 2:15)

Continue in God's Word

Then said Jesus to those Jews which believed on him, If ye continue in my word, then are ye my disciples indeed; And ye shall know the truth, and the truth shall make you free. (John 8:31-32)

Pray Unceasingly

Pray without ceasing. (1Thessalonians 5:17)

Trust in the Lord

I will say of the Lord, He is my refuge and my fortress: my God; in him will I trust. (Psalm 91:2)

Hope Continually

But I will hope continually, and will yet praise thee more and more. (Psalm 71:14)

In Everything Give Thanks

In every thing give thanks: for this is the will of God in Christ Jesus concerning you. (1 Thessalonians 5:18)

Wait on the Lord

But they that wait upon the LORD shall renew their strength; they shall mount up with wings as eagles; they shall run, and not be weary; and they shall walk, and not faint. (Isaiah 40:31)

Rest in the Lord

Come unto me, all ye that labour and are heavy laden, and I will give you rest. Take my yoke upon you, and learn of me; for I am meek and lowly in heart: and ye shall find rest unto your souls. For my yoke is easy, and my burden is light. (Matthew 11:28-30)

Hope and Be Purified

Beloved, now are we the sons of God, and it doth not yet appear what we shall be: but we know that, when he shall appear, we shall be like him; for we shall see him as he is. And every man that hath this hope in him purifieth himself, even as he is pure. (1 John 3:2-3)

Rejoice Evermore

Rejoice evermore. (1Thessalonians 5:16)

Endure To the End

And ye shall be hated of all men for my name's sake: but he that shall endure unto the end, the same shall be saved. (Mark 13:13)

WILT THOU BE MADE WHOLE?

> And a certain man was there, which had an infirmity thirty and eight years. When Jesus saw him lie, and knew that he had been now a long time in that case, he saith unto him, Wilt thou be made whole? (John 5:5-6)

AS HE DID with the man by the pool of Siloam, Jesus asks all who profess to follow Him—"Wilt thou be made whole?" Hymnist William J. Kirkpatrick echoed this when he asked this same question in his 1912 hymn—"Wilt Thou Be Made Whole?"

Hear the footsteps of Jesus,
He is now passing by,
Bearing balm for the wounded,
Healing all who apply;
As he spake to the suff'rer
Who lay at the pool,
He is saying this moment,
"Wilt thou be made whole?"

Wilt thou be made whole?
Wilt thou be made whole?
O come, weary suff'rer,
O come, sin-sick soul;
See, the life-stream is flowing,
See, the cleansing waves roll,
Step into the current,
and thou shalt be whole.

Having Done All to Stand

Soldier of Christ, be steadfast!
This is the "evil day;"
Look to your Royal Leader,
Ever His word obey.
Taking the heav'nly armour,
Wait for your Lord's command;
This is the charge He gives you,
"Having done all, to stand."

Patient and true and faithful,
Facing the deadly foe;
Stand in the place appointed,
March, when He bids you go.
All through the passing moments,
Onward to Canaan's land;
Banish all fear and doubting,
"Having done all, to stand."

This is no time to question,
This is no time to yield;
Never a soul should falter,
Bearing His sword and shield.
Keep in the ranks of Jesus,
Watching on ev'ry hand;
This is the Christian duty,
"Having done all, to stand."

Julia H. Johnston (1891)

7

Standing Fast

> If thou faint in the day of adversity, thy strength is small. (Proverbs 24:10)

Hostility towards those who hold fast to the Lord Jesus Christ and the literal teachings of the Bible has increased greatly. Biblical Christians endeavoring to stand in their faith have been dismayed and saddened at the growing antagonism coming at them not only from the world but from within the professing church itself. This chapter will attempt to convey what Scripture tells us about remaining faithful in the midst of this spiritual opposition—what to expect and how to biblically respond.

STANDING

STANDING IS TO be stationary; to persevere, to endure, to stand fast. While the world moves "forward" with its distorted agenda, God's people are exhorted to *stand fast* in their faith as they *stand against* false teachings and the wiles of the Devil.

> Therefore, brethren, stand fast, and hold the traditions which ye have been taught, whether by word, or our epistle. (2 Thessalonians 2:15)

> Finally, my brethren, be strong in the Lord, and in the power of his might. Put on the whole armour of God, that ye may be able to stand against the wiles of the devil. (Ephesians 6:10-11)

STEADFAST

THE ACT OF standing fast is to be steadfast. Steadfast means firm, fixed, settled, or established. Not changing, fickle or wavering; constant. As believers, we are to remain steadfast and unmoveable in our faith as we resist the Devil and the temptations of the world.

> Therefore, my beloved brethren, be ye stedfast, unmoveable, always abounding in the work of the Lord, forasmuch as ye know that your labour is not in vain in the Lord. (1 Corinthians 15:58)

> But exhort one another daily, while it is called To day; lest any of you be hardened through the deceitfulness of sin. For we are made partakers of Christ, if we hold the beginning of our confidence stedfast unto the end. (Hebrews 3:13-14)

KEEPING

TO KEEP IS to hold fast, preserve, and maintain. We stand fast and remain steadfast by keeping God's Word, keeping His ways, keeping His works, and keeping the faith.

> But he said, Yea rather, blessed are they that hear the word of God, and keep it. (Luke 11:28)

> Jesus answered and said unto him, If a man love me, he will keep my words: and my Father will love him, and we will come unto him, and make our abode with him. (John 14:23)

> Now therefore hearken unto me, O ye children: for blessed are they that keep my ways. (Proverbs 8:32)

> But that which ye have already hold fast till I come. And he that overcometh, and keepeth my works unto the end, to him will I give power over the nations. (Revelation 2:25-26)

CONTINUING

TO CONTINUE IS to stay, abide, remain, stand. We do not change. We do not depart from the faith. We do not fall away from the faith. We continue in the faith.

> Then said Jesus to those Jews which believed on him, If ye continue in my word, then are ye my disciples indeed; And ye shall know the truth, and the truth shall make you free. (John 8:31-32)

> But continue thou in the things which thou hast learned and hast been assured of, knowing of whom thou hast learned them. (2 Timothy 3:14)

> And when they had preached the gospel to that city, and had taught many, they returned again to Lystra, and to Iconium, and Antioch, Confirming the souls of the disciples, and exhorting them to continue in the faith, and that we must through much tribulation enter into the kingdom of God. (Acts 14:21-22)

THE COST

THERE IS A cost that comes with our faithfulness to God and His Word. The price we pay is having to endure the trials, tribulation, and persecution that comes with our faith.

> For which of you, intending to build a tower, sitteth not down first, and counteth the cost, whether he have sufficient to finish it? Lest haply, after he hath laid the foundation, and is not able to finish it, all that behold it begin to mock him, Saying, This man began to build, and was not able to finish it. (Luke 14:28-30)

ENDURING

TO ENDURE IS to remain, to undergo, to bear trials. It is to have fortitude, to persevere, abide, take patiently, suffer.

> But he that shall endure unto the end, the same shall be saved. (Matthew 24:13)

> Behold, we count them happy which endure. (James 5:11)

> Wherefore seeing we also are compassed about with so great a cloud of witnesses, let us lay aside every weight, and the sin which doth so easily beset us, and let us run with patience the race that is set before us, Looking unto Jesus the author and finisher of our faith; who for the joy that was set before him endured the cross, despising the shame, and is set down at the right hand of the throne of God. (Hebrews 12:1-2)

Thanks to God's Word, we know what to expect and how to respond to whatever befalls us. Mercifully, we are given the assurance that with God's help we can endure even the most challenging and difficult trials and temptations.

What to Expect and How to Respond

1) Expect Trouble

> Yet man is born unto trouble, as the sparks fly upward. (Job 5:7)
>
> For nation shall rise against nation, and kingdom against kingdom: and there shall be earthquakes in divers places, and there shall be famines and troubles: these are the beginnings of sorrows. (Mark 13:8)
>
> And at that time shall Michael stand up, the great prince which standeth for the children of thy people: and there shall be a time of trouble, such as never was since there was a nation even to that same time: and at that time thy people shall be delivered, every one that shall be found written in the book. (Daniel 12:1)

Biblical Response

God is our refuge and strength, a very present help in trouble. (Psalm 46:1)

In the day of my trouble I will call upon thee: for thou wilt answer me. (Psalm 86:7)

Let not your heart be troubled: ye believe in God, believe also in me. (John 14:1)

We are troubled on every side, yet not distressed; we are perplexed, but not in despair; Persecuted, but not forsaken; cast down, but not destroyed; Always bearing about in the body the dying of the Lord Jesus, that the life also of Jesus might be made manifest in our body. (2 Corinthians 4:8-10)

And ye shall hear of wars and rumours of wars: see that ye be not troubled: for all these things must come to pass, but the end is not yet. (Matthew 24:6)

Prayer

> The troubles of my heart are enlarged: O bring thou me out of my distresses. (Psalm 25:17)

2) Expect Suffering

> For unto you it is given in the behalf of Christ, not only to believe on him, but also to suffer for his sake. (Philippians 1:29)
>
> For as the sufferings of Christ abound in us, so our consolation also aboundeth by Christ. (2 Corinthians 1:5)

Biblical Response

But rejoice, inasmuch as ye are partakers of Christ's sufferings; that, when his glory shall be revealed, ye may be glad also with exceeding joy. (1 Peter 4:13)

Yet if any man suffer as a Christian, let him not be ashamed; but let him glorify God on this behalf. (1 Peter 4:16)

And if children, then heirs; heirs of God, and joint-heirs with Christ; if so be that we suffer with him, that we may be also glorified together. For I reckon that the sufferings of this present time are not worthy to be compared with the glory which shall be revealed in us. (Romans 8:17-18)

And to him they agreed: and when they had called the apostles, and beaten them, they commanded that they should not speak in the name of Jesus, and let them go. And they departed from the presence of the council, rejoicing that they were counted worthy to suffer shame for his name. (Acts 5:40-41)

For this is thankworthy, if a man for conscience toward God endure grief, suffering wrongfully. For what glory is it, if, when ye be buffeted for your faults, ye shall take it patiently? but if, when ye do well, and suffer for it, ye take it patiently, this is acceptable with God. (1 Peter 2:19-20)

Prayer

Have mercy upon me, O Lord; consider my trouble which I suffer of them that hate me, thou that liftest me up from the gates of death. That I may show forth all thy praise in the gates of the daughter of Zion: I will rejoice in thy salvation. (Psalm 9:13-14)

3) Expect Grief and Sorrow

For in much wisdom is much grief: and he that increaseth knowledge increaseth sorrow. (Ecclesiastes 1:18)

For what hath man of all his labour, and of the vexation of his heart, wherein he hath laboured under the sun? For all his days are sorrows, and his travail grief; yea, his heart taketh not rest in the night. This is also vanity. (Ecclesiastes 2:22-23)

Biblical Response

Blessed are they that mourn: for they shall be comforted. (Matthew 5:4)

Sorrow is better than laughter: for by the sadness of the countenance the heart is made better. The heart of the wise is in the house of mourning; but the heart of fools is in the house of mirth. (Ecclesiastes 7:3-4)

As sorrowful, yet alway rejoicing; as poor, yet making many rich; as having nothing, and yet possessing all things. (2 Corinthians 6:10)

For godly sorrow worketh repentance to salvation not to be repented of: but the sorrow of the world worketh death. (2 Corinthians 7:10)

Prayer

Have mercy upon me, O Lord, for I am in trouble: mine eye is consumed with grief, yea, my soul and my belly. (Psalm 31:9)

4) Expect Persecution

Yea, and all that will live godly in Christ Jesus shall suffer persecution. (2 Timothy 3:12)

> Remember the word that I said unto you, The servant is not greater than his lord. If they have persecuted me, they will also persecute you. (John 15:20)

Biblical Response

Blessed are they which are persecuted for righteousness' sake: for theirs is the kingdom of heaven. Blessed are ye, when men shall revile you, and persecute you, and shall say all manner of evil against you falsely, for my sake. Rejoice, and be exceeding glad: for great is your reward in heaven: for so persecuted they the prophets which were before you. (Matthew 5:10-12)

But I say unto you, Love your enemies, bless them that curse you, do good to them that hate you, and pray for them which despitefully use you, and persecute you. (Matthew 5:44)

Therefore I take pleasure in infirmities, in reproaches, in necessities, in persecutions, in distresses for Christ's sake: for when I am weak, then am I strong. (2 Corinthians 12:10)

Princes have persecuted me without a cause: but my heart standeth in awe of thy word. I rejoice at thy word, as one that findeth great spoil. (Psalm 119:161-162)

Prayer

> O Lord my God, in thee do I put my trust: save me from all them that persecute me, and deliver me. (Psalm 7:1)

5) Expect Affliction

Many are the afflictions of the righteous: but the LORD delivereth him out of them all. (Psalm 34:19)

That no man should be moved by these afflictions: for yourselves know that we are appointed thereunto. (1 Thessalonians 3:3)

For in those days shall be affliction, such as was not from the beginning of the creation which God created unto this time, neither shall be. (Mark 13:19)

Biblical Response

For which cause we faint not; but though our outward man perish, yet the inward man is renewed day by day. For our light affliction, which is but for a moment, worketh for us a far more exceeding and eternal weight of glory. (2 Corinthians 4:16-17)

This is my comfort in my affliction: for thy word hath quickened me. (Psalm 119:50)

It is good for me that I have been afflicted; that I might learn thy statutes. (Psalm 119:71)

Prayer

Turn thee unto me, and have mercy upon me; for I am desolate and afflicted. (Psalm 25:16)

6) Expect Tribulation

> Confirming the souls of the disciples, and exhorting them to continue in the faith, and that we must through much tribulation enter into the kingdom of God. (Acts 14:22)

Biblical Response

When thou art in tribulation, and all these things are come upon thee, even in the latter days, if thou turn to the LORD thy God, and shalt be obedient unto his voice; (For the LORD thy God is a merciful God;) he will not forsake thee, neither destroy thee, nor forget the covenant of thy fathers which he sware unto them. (Deuteronomy 4:30-31)

These things I have spoken unto you, that in me ye might have peace. In the world ye shall have tribulation: but be of good cheer; I have overcome the world. (John 16:33)

Blessed be God, even the Father of our Lord Jesus Christ, the Father of mercies, and the God of all comfort; Who comforteth us in all our tribulation, that we may be able to comfort them which are in any trouble, by the comfort wherewith we ourselves are comforted of God. (2 Corinthians 1:3-4)

And not only so, but we glory in tribulations also: knowing that tribulation worketh patience; And patience, experience; and experience, hope. (Romans 5:3-4)

Great is my boldness of speech toward you, great is my glorying of you: I am filled with comfort, I am exceeding joyful in all our tribulation. (2 Corinthians 7:4)

Rejoicing in hope; patient in tribulation; continuing instant in prayer. (Romans 12:12)

Prayer

And, behold, as thy life was much set by this day in mine eyes, so let my life be much set by in the eyes of the LORD, and let him deliver me out of all tribulation. (1 Samuel 26:24)

7) Expect Temptation

There hath no temptation taken you but such as is common to man: but God is faithful, who will not suffer you to be tempted above that ye are able; but will with the temptation also make a way to escape, that ye may be able to bear it. (1 Corinthians 10:13)

Because thou hast kept the word of my patience, I also will keep thee from the hour of temptation, which shall come upon all the world, to try them that dwell upon the earth. (Revelation 3:10)

Biblical Response

Watch and pray, that ye enter not into temptation: the spirit indeed is willing, but the flesh is weak. (Matthew 26:41)

My brethren, count it all joy when ye fall into divers temptations; Knowing this, that the trying of your faith worketh patience. (James 1:2-3)

Blessed is the man that endureth temptation: for when he is tried, he shall receive the crown of life, which the Lord hath promised to them that love him. (James 1:12)

Prayer

And lead us not into temptation, but deliver us from evil: For thine is the kingdom, and the power, and the glory, for ever. Amen. (Matthew 6:13)

8) Expect Trials

That the trial of your faith, being much more precious than of gold that perisheth, though it be tried with fire, might be found unto praise and honour and glory at the appearing of Jesus Christ: Whom having not seen, ye love; in whom, though now ye see him not, yet believing, ye rejoice with joy unspeakable and full of glory. (1 Peter 1:7-8)

Biblical Response

Beloved, think it not strange concerning the fiery trial which is to try you, as though some strange thing happened unto you: But rejoice, inasmuch as ye are partakers of Christ's sufferings; that, when his glory shall be revealed, ye may be glad also with exceeding joy. (1 Peter 4:12-13)

Prayer

O keep my soul, and deliver me: let me not be ashamed; for I put my trust in thee. (Psalm 25:20)

9) Expect Hatred

Marvel not, my brethren, if the world hate you. (1 John 3:13)

And ye shall be hated of all men for my name's sake. (Luke 21:17)

> Then shall they deliver you up to be afflicted, and shall kill you: and ye shall be hated of all nations for my name's sake. (Matthew 24:9)

Biblical Response

Blessed are ye, when men shall hate you, and when they shall separate you from their company, and shall reproach you, and cast out your name as evil, for the Son of man's sake. Rejoice ye in that day, and leap for joy: for, behold, your reward is great in heaven: for in the like manner did their fathers unto the prophets. (Luke 6:22-23)

But I say unto you, Love your enemies, bless them that curse you, do good to them that hate you, and pray for them which despitefully use you, and persecute you. (Matthew 5:44)

Prayer

> Deliver me out of the mire, and let me not sink: let me be delivered from them that hate me, and out of the deep waters. (Psalm 69:14)

10) Expect to be Called Beelzebub/Satan

> It is enough for the disciple that he be as his master, and the servant as his lord. If they have called the master of the house Beelzebub, how much more shall they call them of his household? (Matthew 10:25)

Biblical Response

Blessed are ye, when men shall revile you, and persecute you, and shall say all manner of evil against you falsely, for my sake. Rejoice, and be exceeding glad: for great is your reward in heaven: for so persecuted they the prophets which were before you. (Matthew 5:11-12)

Bless them which persecute you: bless, and curse not. (Romans 12:14)

And labour, working with our own hands: being reviled, we bless; being persecuted, we suffer it: Being defamed, we entreat: we are made as the filth of the world, and are the offscouring of all things unto this day. (1 Corinthians 4:12-13)

Prayer

My times are in thy hand: deliver me from the hand of mine enemies, and from them that persecute me. (Psalm 31:15)

11) Expect You May Die for Your Faith

Yea, for thy sake are we killed all the day long; we are counted as sheep for the slaughter. (Psalm 44:22)

These things have I spoken unto you, that ye should not be offended. They shall put you out of the synagogues: yea, the time cometh, that whosoever killeth you will think that he doeth God service. (John 16:1-2)

Then shall they deliver you up to be afflicted, and shall kill you: and ye shall be hated of all nations for my name's sake. (Matthew 24:9)

Biblical Response

And fear not them which kill the body, but are not able to kill the soul: but rather fear him which is able to destroy both soul and body in hell. (Matthew 10:28)

Fear none of those things which thou shalt suffer . . . be thou faithful unto death, and I will give thee a crown of life. (Revelation 2:10)

Precious in the sight of the LORD is the death of his saints. (Psalm 116:15)

For this God is our God for ever and ever: he will be our guide even unto death. (Psalm 48:14)

And they overcame him by the blood of the Lamb, and by the word of their testimony; and they loved not their lives unto the death. (Revelation 12:11)

Prayer

Yea, though I walk through the valley of the shadow of death, I will fear no evil: for thou art with me; thy rod and thy staff they comfort me. (Psalm 23:4)

12) Expect to See Jesus

Looking for that blessed hope, and the glorious appearing of the great God and our Saviour Jesus Christ. (Titus 2:13)

Behold, he cometh with clouds; and every eye shall see him, and they also which pierced him: and all kindreds of the earth shall wail because of him. (Revelation 1:7)

> For as the lightning cometh out of the east, and shineth even unto the west; so shall also the coming of the Son of man be. (Matthew 24:27)

Biblical Response

Blessed are those servants, whom the lord when he cometh shall find watching. (Luke 12:37)

And there shall be signs in the sun, and in the moon, and in the stars; and upon the earth distress of nations, with perplexity; the sea and the waves roaring; Men's hearts failing them for fear, and for looking after those things which are coming on the earth: for the powers of heaven shall be shaken. And then shall they see the Son of man coming in a cloud with power and great glory. And when these things begin to come to pass, then look up, and lift up your heads; for your redemption draweth nigh. (Luke 21:25-28)

For the Lord himself shall descend from heaven with a shout, with the voice of the archangel, and with the trump of God: and the dead in Christ shall rise first: Then we which are alive and remain shall be caught up together with them in the clouds, to meet the Lord in the air: and so shall we ever be with the Lord. Wherefore comfort one another with these words. (1Thessalonians 4:16-18)

Be ye therefore ready also: for the Son of man cometh at an hour when ye think not. (Luke 12:40)

Prayer

> He which testifieth these things saith, Surely I come quickly. Amen. Even so, come, Lord Jesus. (Revelation 22:20)

13) Expect a New Heaven and a New Earth

> And I saw a new heaven and a new earth: for the first heaven and the first earth were passed away; and there was no more sea. And I John saw the holy city, new Jerusalem, coming down from God out of heaven, prepared as a bride adorned for her husband. (Revelation 21:1-2)

Biblical Response

He that overcometh shall inherit all things; and I will be his God, and he shall be my son. (Revelation 21:7)

Prayer

> Now unto him that is able to do exceeding abundantly above all that we ask or think, according to the power that worketh in us, Unto him be glory in the church by Christ Jesus throughout all ages, world without end. Amen. (Ephesians 3:20-21)

REJOICE, GIVE THANKS, GLORIFY GOD, EXHORT ONE ANOTHER

LIFE CAN BE extremely difficult and challenging. It is not easy being a biblical Christian. Even if we continue in His Word and remain steadfast in our faith, we are promised trials and tribulation. We know that we will be mocked, hated, betrayed, persecuted, and maybe even killed for our faith. But we are not to be deterred by a world and an apostate church that would seek to undo our testimony. Even in our most trying moments, we are encouraged to rejoice and be thankful as we glorify God and exhort one another daily to be steadfast in our faith until the very end:

> Rejoice evermore. (1 Thessalonians 5:16)

> In every thing give thanks: for this is the will of God in Christ Jesus concerning you. (1 Thessalonians 5:18)

> I will praise thee, O Lord my God, with all my heart: and I will glorify thy name for evermore. (Psalm 86:12)

> But exhort one another daily, while it is called To day; lest any of you be hardened through the deceitfulness of sin. For we are made partakers of Christ, if we hold the beginning of our confidence stedfast unto the end. (Hebrews 3:13-14)

OVERCOMER

TO OVERCOME IS to subdue, conquer, prevail, to get the victory. Overcomers do not fall away. We are to be more than conquerors—we are to be overcomers. Paul said:

> Nay, in all these things we are more than conquerors through him that loved us. For I am persuaded, that neither death, nor life, nor angels, nor principalities, nor powers, nor things present, nor things to come, Nor height, nor depth, nor any other creature, shall be able to separate us from the love of God, which is in Christ Jesus our Lord. (Romans 8:37-39)

Jesus said:

> To him that overcometh will I grant to sit with me in my throne, even as I also overcame, and am set down with my Father in his throne. (Revelation 3:21)

ENDURE AND FLOURISH

WHEN WE GROW weary and feel faint, we must remember that our strength comes from the Lord. He will renew us for the task at hand. His grace is sufficient, and He perfects His strength in our weakness. As we are strengthened and encouraged, we must encourage others that God's Word is true and that His truth will prevail in the end. Evil will be vanquished, and those that are planted in the house of the Lord will flourish in the courts of our God.

> When the wicked spring as the grass, and when all the workers of iniquity do flourish; it is that they shall be destroyed for ever: But thou, LORD, art most high for evermore. For, lo, thine enemies, O LORD, for, lo, thine enemies shall perish; all the workers of iniquity shall be scattered. . . . Mine eye also shall see my desire on mine enemies, and mine ears shall hear my desire of the wicked that rise up against me. The righteous shall flourish like the palm tree: he shall grow like a cedar in Lebanon. Those that be planted in the house of the LORD shall flourish in the courts of our God. (Psalm 92:7-9, 11-13)

8

Beware

> Beware therefore, lest that come upon you, which is spoken of in the prophets. (Acts 13:40)

BEWARE YET REJOICE

Scripture tells us to rejoice always (Philippians 4:4), to rejoice right to the end (Hebrews 3:6), and to rejoice evermore (1 Thessalonians 5:16). But the Bible also reminds us to "take heed" and "beware" of a great many things. And while we must be ever-mindful of our Spiritual Adversary (1 Peter 5:8) and his many devices (2 Corinthians 2:11), we still should always be rejoicing in our heart of hearts for what God has done for us through our Lord and Savior Jesus Christ.

In Paul's letter to the Philippians he mentions rejoicing eleven separate times. However, in the midst of his exhortations, he also warns them to "beware of evil workers" (Philippians 3:2). For all intents and purposes, "rejoice but beware" is an underlying theme of our Christian faith. In fact, the Bible makes it clear that these two concepts are inextricably intertwined.

And while we are to rejoice always, Scripture is clear that always rejoicing and never being watchful can result in subtle compromise, great deception, and even the loss of one's faith. In Revelation 3:1-3 the Lord warns about those who have a reputation for great rejoicing and revival—who *seem* to be spiritually alive—when, in reality, they are spiritually dead. He exhorts them to take heed and beware—to be watchful, to strengthen the things which remain, to remember what they have received and heard, to hold fast and repent. The following Bible verses are some of the many warnings to take heed and beware of as we press on to the higher calling of our Lord.

BEWARE

150 SELECTED VERSES

— OLD TESTAMENT WARNINGS —

Beware of the Tempter and Doubting God's Word

Now the serpent was more subtle than any beast of the field which the LORD God had made. And he said unto the woman, Yea, hath God said, Ye shall not eat of every tree of the garden? (Genesis 3:1)

Beware of Worldly Oneness

And the LORD said, Behold, the people is one, and they have all one language; and this they begin to do: and now nothing will be restrained from them, which they have imagined to do. (Genesis 11:6)

Beware of Counterfeit Miracles

Then Pharaoh also called the wise men and the sorcerers: now the magicians of Egypt, they also did in like manner with their enchantments. (Exodus 7:11)

Beware of Those With Familiar Spirits

Regard not them that have familiar spirits, neither seek after wizards, to be defiled by them: I am the LORD your God. (Leviticus 19:31)

Beware of Graven Images and Other Likenesses of God

Take heed unto yourselves, lest ye forget the covenant of the LORD your God, which he made with you, and make you a graven image, or the likeness of any thing, which the LORD thy God hath forbidden thee. (Deuteronomy 4:23)

Beware of Deceptive Signs and Wonders

If there arise among you a prophet, or a dreamer of dreams, and giveth thee a sign or a wonder, And the sign or the wonder come to pass, whereof he spake unto thee, saying, Let us go after other gods, which thou hast not known, and let us serve them; Thou shalt not hearken unto the words of that prophet, or that dreamer of dreams: for the LORD your God proveth you, to know whether ye love the LORD your God with all your heart and with all your soul. (Deuteronomy 13:1-3)

Beware of Evil in the Latter Days

For I know that after my [Moses] death ye will utterly corrupt yourselves, and turn aside from the way which I have commanded you; and evil will befall you in the latter days; because ye will do evil in the sight of the LORD, to provoke him to anger through the work of your hands. (Deuteronomy 31:29)

Beware of Ungodly Counsel

Blessed is the man that walketh not in the counsel of the ungodly, nor standeth in the way of sinners, nor sitteth in the seat of the scornful. (Psalm 1:1)

Beware of Flatterers and the Double Hearted

They speak vanity every one with his neighbour: with flattering lips and with a double heart do they speak. (Psalm 12:2)

Beware When the Vilest Men are Exalted

The wicked walk on every side, when the vilest men are exalted. (Psalm 12:8)

Beware of Your Own Vanity

Behold, thou hast made my days as an handbreadth; and mine age is as nothing before thee: verily every man at his best state is altogether vanity. (Psalm 39:5)

Beware of Reincarnation

For he remembered that they were but flesh; a wind that passeth away, and cometh not again. (Psalm 78:39)

Beware of Ungodly Spiritual Manifestations

They reel to and fro, and stagger like a drunken man, and are at their wit's end. (Psalm 107:27)

Beware of the Right Hand of Falsehood

Rid me, and deliver me from the hand of strange children, whose mouth speaketh vanity, and their right hand is a right hand of falsehood. (Psalm 144:11)

Beware of Contrived Unity

Though hand join in hand, the wicked shall not be unpunished: but the seed of the righteous shall be delivered. (Proverbs 11:21)

Beware of a Way That Seems Right

There is a way which seemeth right unto a man, but the end thereof are the ways of death. (Proverbs 14:12)

Beware of Self–Deceit

All the ways of a man are clean in his own eyes; but the LORD weigheth the spirits. (Proverbs 16:2)

Beware of Pride

Pride goeth before destruction, and an haughty spirit before a fall. (Proverbs 16:18)

Beware of Fainting in the Day of Adversity

If thou faint in the day of adversity, thy strength is small. (Proverbs 24:10)

Beware of Change Agents

My son, fear thou the LORD and the king: and meddle not with them that are given to change. (Proverbs 24:21)

Beware of Having No Self–Control

He that hath no rule over his own spirit is like a city that is broken down, and without walls. (Proverbs 25:28)

Beware of Trusting Your Heart

He that trusteth in his own heart is a fool: but whoso walketh wisely, he shall be delivered. (Proverbs 28:26)

Beware of Those Who Add to God's Word

Every word of God is pure: he is a shield unto them that put their trust in him. Add thou not unto his words, lest he reprove thee, and thou be found a liar. (Proverbs 30:5-6)

Beware of Leaders Who Mislead

O my people, they which lead thee cause thee to err, and destroy the way of thy paths. (Isaiah 3:12)

Beware of "Wild Grapes"

What could have been done more to my vineyard, that I have not done in it? wherefore, when I looked that it should bring forth grapes, brought it forth wild grapes? (Isaiah 5:4)

Beware of Ungodly Rejoicing

Therefore hell hath enlarged herself, and opened her mouth without measure: and their glory, and their multitude, and their pomp, and he that rejoiceth, shall descend into it. (Isaiah 5:14)

Beware of Those Who Call Evil Good

Woe unto them that call evil good, and good evil; that put darkness for light, and light for darkness; that put bitter for sweet, and sweet for bitter! (Isaiah 5:20)

Beware of Ungodly Associations

Associate yourselves, O ye people, and ye shall be broken in pieces; and give ear, all ye of far countries: gird yourselves, and ye shall be broken in pieces; gird yourselves, and ye shall be broken in pieces. Take counsel together, and it shall come to nought; speak the word, and it shall not stand: for God is with us. (Isaiah 8:9-10)

Beware of Strange Slips

Because thou hast forgotten the God of thy salvation, and hast not been mindful of the rock of thy strength, therefore shalt thou plant pleasant plants, and shalt set it with strange slips: In the day shalt thou make thy plant to grow, and in the morning shalt thou make thy seed to flourish: but the harvest shall be a heap in the day of grief and of desperate sorrow. (Isaiah 17:10-11)

Beware of Those Wanting to Hear Smooth Things

That this is a rebellious people, lying children, children that will not hear the law of the LORD: Which say to the seers, See not; and to the prophets, Prophesy not unto us right things, speak unto us smooth things, prophesy deceits: Get you out of the way, turn aside out of the path, cause the Holy One of Israel to cease from before us. (Isaiah 30:9-11)

Beware of Those Mentioning God but Not in Truth

Hear ye this, O house of Jacob, which are called by the name of Israel, and are come forth out of the waters of Judah, which swear by the name of the LORD, and make mention of the God of Israel, but not in truth, nor in righteousness. (Isaiah 48:1)

Beware of Worldly Unity

Behold, they shall surely gather together, but not by me. (Isaiah 54:15)

Beware of Men's Thoughts and Ways

For my thoughts are not your thoughts, neither are your ways my ways, saith the LORD. For as the heavens are higher than the earth, so are my ways higher than your ways, and my thoughts than your thoughts. (Isaiah 55:8-9)

Beware of Blind Watchmen

His watchmen are blind: they are all ignorant, they are all dumb dogs, they cannot bark; sleeping, lying down, loving to slumber. Yea, they are greedy dogs which can never have enough, and they are shepherds that cannot understand: they all look to their own way, every one for his gain, from his quarter. (Isaiah 56:10-11)

Beware of Men's Snares and Traps

For among my people are found wicked men: they lay wait, as he that setteth snares; they set a trap, they catch men. (Jeremiah 5:26)

Beware: "Horrible" Things Can Seem "Wonderful"

A wonderful and horrible thing is committed in the land; The prophets prophesy falsely, and the priests bear rule by their means; and my people love to have it so: and what will ye do in the end thereof? (Jeremiah 5:30-31)

Beware of Grievous Revolters

They are all grievous revolters, walking with slanders: they are brass and iron; they are all corrupters. (Jeremiah 6:28)

Beware of Trusting Lying Words

Trust ye not in lying words, saying, The temple of the LORD, The temple of the LORD, The temple of the LORD, are these. (Jeremiah 7:4)

Beware of Not Recognizing God's Judgment

Yea, the stork in the heaven knoweth her appointed times; and the turtle and the crane and the swallow observe the time of their coming; but my people know not the judgment of the LORD. (Jeremiah 8:7)

Beware of Those Who Are Not Valiant For the Truth

And they bend their tongues like their bow for lies: but they are not valiant for the truth upon the earth; for they proceed from evil to evil, and they know not me, saith the LORD. (Jeremiah 9:3)

Beware of Conspiracies That Are Real

And the LORD said unto me, A conspiracy is found among the men of Judah, and among the inhabitants of Jerusalem. (Jeremiah 11:9)

Beware of Men's Lip Service

Thou hast planted them, yea, they have taken root: they grow, yea, they bring forth fruit: thou art near in their mouth, and far from their reins. (Jeremiah 12:2)

Beware of Being Unprepared

If thou hast run with the footmen, and they have wearied thee, then how canst thou contend with horses? and if in the land of peace, wherein thou trustedst, they wearied thee, then how wilt thou do in the swelling of Jordan? (Jeremiah 12:5)

Beware of Pastors Who Are Destroying God's Vineyard

Many pastors have destroyed my vineyard, they have trodden my portion under foot, they have made my pleasant portion a desolate wilderness. (Jeremiah 12:10)

Beware of Spiritual Drunkenness

Then shalt thou say unto them, Thus saith the LORD, Behold, I will fill all the inhabitants of this land, even the kings that sit upon David's throne, and the priests, and the prophets, and all the inhabitants of Jerusalem, with drunkenness. (Jeremiah 13:13)

Beware of Trusting in Falsehoods

This is thy lot, the portion of thy measures from me, saith the LORD; because thou hast forgotten me, and trusted in falsehood. (Jeremiah 13:25)

Beware of Spiritual Wandering

Thus saith the LORD unto this people, Thus have they loved to wander, they have not refrained their feet, therefore the LORD doth not accept them; he will now remember their iniquity, and visit their sins. (Jeremiah 14:10)

Beware of False Prophets With False Visions

Then the LORD said unto me, The prophets prophesy lies in my name: I sent them not, neither have I commanded them, neither spake unto them: they prophesy unto you a false vision and divination, and a thing of nought, and the deceit of their heart. (Jeremiah 14:14)

Beware of Putting Your Trust in Man

Thus saith the LORD; Cursed be the man that trusteth in man, and maketh flesh his arm, and whose heart departeth from the LORD. (Jeremiah 17:5)

Beware of Your Own Heart

The heart is deceitful above all things, and desperately wicked: who can know it? (Jeremiah 17:9)

Beware of the Lord's Anger in the Latter Days

The anger of the LORD shall not return, until he have executed, and till he have performed the thoughts of his heart: in the latter days ye shall consider it perfectly. (Jeremiah 23:20)

Beware of False Prophets

I have not sent these prophets, yet they ran: I have not spoken to them, yet they prophesied. But if they had stood in my counsel, and had caused my people to hear my words, then they should have turned them from their evil way, and from the evil of their doings. (Jeremiah 23:21-22)

Beware of False Dreams

Behold, I am against them that prophesy false dreams, saith the LORD, and do tell them, and cause my people to err by their lies, and by their lightness; yet I sent them not, nor commanded them: therefore they shall not profit this people at all, saith the LORD. (Jeremiah 23:32)

Beware of Men Doing the Lord's Work Deceitfully

Cursed be he that doeth the work of the LORD deceitfully, and cursed be he that keepeth back his sword from blood. (Jeremiah 48:10)

Beware of Men Thinking They Are God

Son of man, say unto the prince of Tyrus, Thus saith the Lord GOD; Because thine heart is lifted up, and thou hast said, I am a God, I sit in the seat of God, in the midst of the seas; yet thou art a man, and not God, though thou set thine heart as the heart of God. (Ezekiel 28:2)

Beware When the Whole World Rejoices

When the whole earth rejoiceth, I will make thee desolate. (Ezekiel 35:13-14)

Beware of Antichrist's Coming Kingdom

Thus he said, The fourth beast shall be the fourth kingdom upon earth, which shall be diverse from all kingdoms, and shall devour the whole earth, and shall tread it down, and break it in pieces. (Daniel 7:23)

Beware of Antichrist's Blasphemies and Changes

And he shall speak great words against the most High, and shall wear out the saints of the most High, and think to change times and laws: and they shall be given into his hand until a time and times and the dividing of time. (Daniel 7:25)

Beware That Antichrist Will "Destroy Wonderfully"

And in the latter time of their kingdom, when the transgressors are come to the full, a king of fierce countenance, and understanding dark sentences, shall stand up. And his power shall be mighty, but not by his own power: and he shall destroy wonderfully, and shall prosper, and practice, and shall destroy the mighty and the holy people. (Daniel 8:23-24)

Beware That Antichrist Will Use Peace to Destroy

And through his policy also he shall cause craft to prosper in his hand; and he shall magnify himself in his heart, and by peace shall destroy many: he shall also stand up against the Prince of princes; but he shall be broken without hand. (Daniel 8:25)

Beware of Having a Lack of Knowledge

My people are destroyed for lack of knowledge. (Hosea 4:6)

Beware of a "Return" That Is Not to the True God

They return, but not to the most High. (Hosea 7:16)

Beware of a Famine for Hearing God's Word

Behold, the days come, saith the Lord GOD, that I will send a famine in the land, not a famine of bread, nor a thirst for water, but of hearing the words of the LORD. (Amos 8:11)

Beware of Who You Trust

Trust ye not in a friend, put ye not confidence in a guide. (Micah 7:5)

— NEW TESTAMENT WARNINGS —

Beware of Praying Repetitive Prayers

But when ye pray, use not vain repetitions, as the heathen do: for they think that they shall be heard for their much speaking. (Matthew 6:7)

Beware of Not Forgiving Others

But if ye forgive not men their trespasses, neither will your Father forgive your trespasses. (Matthew 6:15)

Beware of Serving Two Masters

No man can serve two masters: for either he will hate the one, and love the other; or else he will hold to the one, and despise the other. Ye cannot serve God and mammon. (Matthew 6:24)

Beware of the Log in Your Own Eye

Thou hypocrite, first cast out the beam out of thine own eye; and then shalt thou see clearly to cast out the mote out of thy brother's eye. (Matthew 7:5)

Beware of Casting Your Pearls Before Swine

Give not that which is holy unto the dogs, neither cast ye your pearls before swine, lest they trample them under their feet, and turn again and rend you. (Matthew 7:6)

Beware of the Broad Way

Enter ye in at the strait gate: for wide is the gate, and broad is the way, that leadeth to destruction, and many there be which go in thereat: Because strait is the gate, and narrow is the way, which leadeth unto life, and few there be that find it. (Matthew 7:13-14)

Beware of Wolves in Sheep's Clothing

Beware of false prophets, which come to you in sheep's clothing, but inwardly they are ravening wolves. (Matthew 7:15)

Beware of Not Doing God's Will

Not every one that saith unto me, Lord, Lord, shall enter into the kingdom of heaven; but he that doeth the will of my Father which is in heaven. (Matthew 7:21)

Beware of Men

But beware of men: for they will deliver you up to the councils, and they will scourge you in their synagogues. (Matthew 10:17)

Beware That Men Will Hate You

And ye shall be hated of all men for my name's sake: but he that endureth to the end shall be saved. (Matthew 10:22)

Beware of Enemies in Your Own Household

And a man's foes shall be they of his own household. (Matthew 10:36)

Beware of Hearing but Not Understanding

When any one heareth the word of the kingdom, and understandeth it not, then cometh the wicked one, and catcheth away that which was sown in his heart. This is he which received seed by the way side. (Matthew 13:19)

Beware of Having No Spiritual Depth

But he that received the seed into stony places, the same is he that heareth the word, and anon with joy receiveth it; Yet hath he not root in himself, but dureth for a while: for when tribulation or persecution ariseth because of the word, by and by he is offended. (Matthew 13:20-21)

Beware of Deceitful Riches and Worldly Cares

He also that received seed among the thorns is he that heareth the word; and the care of this world, and the deceitfulness of riches, choke the word, and he becometh unfruitful. (Matthew 13:22)

Beware of Counterfeit Believers

But while men slept, his enemy came and sowed tares among the wheat, and went his way. (Matthew 13:25)

Beware of Undiscerning Leaders

O ye hypocrites, ye can discern the face of the sky; but can ye not discern the signs of the times? (Matthew 16:3)

Beware of Seeking Signs

A wicked and adulterous generation seeketh after a sign; and there shall no sign be given unto it, but the sign of the prophet Jonas. (Matthew 16:4)

Beware of Men's Doctrine

Then understood they how that he bade them not beware of the leaven of bread, but of the doctrine of the Pharisees and of the Sadducees. (Matthew 16:12)

Beware of False Christs

And as he sat upon the mount of Olives, the disciples came unto him privately, saying, Tell us, when shall these things be? and what shall be the sign of thy coming, and of the end of the world? And Jesus answered and said unto them, Take heed that no man deceive you. For many shall come in my name, saying, I am Christ; and shall deceive many. (Matthew 24:3-5)

Beware of False Signs and Wonders

For false Christs and false prophets shall rise, and shall show signs and wonders, to seduce, if it were possible, even the elect. (Mark 13:22)

Beware When Men Speak Well of You

Woe unto you, when all men shall speak well of you! for so did their fathers to the false prophets. (Luke 6:26)

Beware of a Light That Is Dark

Take heed therefore that the light which is in thee be not darkness. (Luke 11:35)

Beware of Hearing but Not Doing

But he that heareth, and doeth not, is like a man that without a foundation built an house upon the earth; against which the stream did beat vehemently, and immediately it fell; and the ruin of that house was great. (Luke 6:49)

Beware of Not Counting the Cost

For which of you, intending to build a tower, sitteth not down first, and counteth the cost, whether he have sufficient to finish it? Lest haply, after he hath laid the foundation, and is not able to finish it, all that behold it begin to mock him, Saying, this man began to build, and was not able to finish. (Luke 14:28-30)

Beware of Being Betrayed by Friends and Family

And ye shall be betrayed both by parents, and brethren, and kinsfolks, and friends; and some of you shall they cause to be put to death. (Luke 21:16)

Beware of What You Are Being Told and Taught

These were more noble than those in Thessalonica, in that they received the word with all readiness of mind, and searched the scriptures daily, whether those things were so. (Acts 17:11)

Beware of Those Not Preaching All the Counsel of God

For I have not shunned to declare unto you all the counsel of God. (Acts 20:27)

Beware of Ungodly Zeal

For I bear them record that they have a zeal of God, but not according to knowledge. (Romans 10:2)

Beware of Grievous Wolves in the Church

For I know this, that after my departing shall grievous wolves enter in among you, not sparing the flock. (Acts 20:29)

Beware of Being Conformed to the World

And be not conformed to this world: but be ye transformed by the renewing of your mind, that ye may prove what is that good, and acceptable, and perfect, will of God. (Romans 12:2)

Beware of Those With Contrary Doctrine

Now I beseech you, brethren, mark them which cause divisions and offences contrary to the doctrine which ye have learned; and avoid them. (Romans 16:17)

Beware of Enticing Words and Men's Wisdom

And my speech and my preaching was not with enticing words of man's wisdom, but in demonstration of the Spirit and of power: That your faith should not stand in the wisdom of men, but in the power of God. (1 Corinthians 2:4-5)

Beware of Other Gods

For though there be that are called gods, whether in heaven or in earth, (as there be gods many, and lords many,) But to us there is but one God, the Father, of whom are all things, and we in him; and one Lord Jesus Christ, by whom are all things, and we by him. (1 Corinthians 8:5-6)

Beware of Falling

Wherefore let him that thinketh he standeth take heed lest he fall. (1 Corinthians 10:12)

Beware of Drinking From Two Cups, Eating From Two Tables

Ye cannot drink the cup of the Lord, and the cup of devils: ye cannot be partakers of the Lord's table, and of the table of devils. (1 Corinthians 10:21)

Beware of Heresies That Will Prove You

For there must be also heresies among you, that they which are approved may be made manifest among you. (1 Corinthians 11:19)

Beware When No Warnings are Given

For if the trumpet give an uncertain sound, who shall prepare himself to the battle? (1 Corinthians 14:8)

Beware of Being Ignorant of Satan's Schemes

Lest Satan should get an advantage of us: for we are not ignorant of his devices. (2 Corinthians 2:11)

Beware of Men Who Deceitfully Handle God's Word

But have renounced the hidden things of dishonesty, not walking in craftiness, nor handling the word of God deceitfully; but by manifestation of the truth commending ourselves to every man's conscience in the sight of God. (2 Corinthians 4:2)

Beware of Being Unequally Yoked

Be ye not unequally yoked together with unbelievers: for what fellowship hath righteousness with unrighteousness? and what communion hath light with darkness? (2 Corinthians 6:14)

Beware of Evil Imaginations and Thoughts

Casting down imaginations, and every high thing that exalteth itself against the knowledge of God, and bringing into captivity every thought to the obedience of Christ. (2 Corinthians 10:5)

Beware of Another Jesus

For if he that cometh preacheth another Jesus, whom we have not preached, or if ye receive another spirit, which ye have not received, or another gospel, which ye have not accepted, ye might well bear with him. (2 Corinthians 11:4)

Beware of False Apostles And Deceitful Workers

For such are false apostles, deceitful workers, transforming themselves into the apostles of Christ. (2 Corinthians 11:13)

Beware That Satan Comes as an Angel of Light

And no marvel; for Satan himself is transformed into an angel of light. Therefore it is no great thing if his ministers also be transformed as the ministers of righteousness; whose end shall be according to their works. (2 Corinthians 11:14-15)

Beware of Pleasing Men Rather Than God

For do I now persuade men, or God? or do I seek to please men? for if I yet pleased men, I should not be the servant of Christ. (Galatians 1:10)

Beware of False Brethren

And that because of false brethren unawares brought in, who came in privily to spy out our liberty which we have in Christ Jesus, that they might bring us into bondage. (Galatians 2:4)

Beware of a Little Leaven

Ye did run well; who did hinder you that ye should not obey the truth? This persuasion cometh not of him that calleth you. A little leaven leaveneth the whole lump. (Galatians 5:7-9)

Beware of Thinking You Are Something

For if a man think himself to be something, when he is nothing, he deceiveth himself. (Galatians 6:3)

Beware of False Doctrines and the Sleight of Men

That we henceforth be no more children, tossed to and fro, and carried about with every wind of doctrine, by the sleight of men, and cunning craftiness, whereby they lie in wait to deceive. (Ephesians 4:14)

Beware of Giving Place to the Devil

Neither give place to the devil. (Ephesians 4:27)

Beware of Fellowshiping With Works of Darkness

And have no fellowship with the unfruitful works of darkness, but rather reprove them. (Ephesians 5:11)

Beware of "Believers" Who Are Actually Enemies

For many walk, of whom I have told you often, and now tell you even weeping, that they are the enemies of the cross of Christ. (Philippians 3:18)

Beware of Men's Philosophy and Tradition

Beware lest any man spoil you through philosophy and vain deceit, after the tradition of men, after the rudiments of the world, and not after Christ. (Colossians 2:8)

Beware of a Deceptive Peace and Safety

For when they shall say, Peace and safety; then sudden destruction cometh upon them, as travail upon a woman with child; and they shall not escape. But ye, brethren, are not in darkness, that that day should overtake you as a thief. (1Thessalonians 5:3-4)

Beware of Satan's Lying Signs and Wonders

Even him, whose coming is after the working of Satan with all power and signs and lying wonders. (2 Thessalonians 2:9)

Beware of Those Who Don't Love the Truth

And with all deceivableness of unrighteousness in them that perish; because they received not the love of the truth, that they might be saved. (2 Thessalonians 2:10)

Beware of Those Who are Doubletongued

Likewise must the deacons be grave, not double-tongued, not given to much wine, not greedy of filthy lucre. (1 Timothy 3:8)

Beware of Seducing Spirits and Doctrines of Devils

Now the Spirit speaketh expressly, that in the latter times some shall depart from the faith, giving heed to seducing spirits, and doctrines of devils. (1 Timothy 4:1)

Beware of the Love of Money

For the love of money is the root of all evil: which while some coveted after, they have erred from the faith, and pierced themselves through with many sorrows. (1 Timothy 6:10)

Beware of Science Falsely So Called

O Timothy, keep that which is committed to thy trust, avoiding profane and vain babblings, and oppositions of science falsely so called: Which some professing have erred concerning the faith. (1 Timothy 6:20-21)

Beware of Being Fearful

For God hath not given us the spirit of fear; but of power, and of love, and of a sound mind. (2 Timothy 1:7)

Beware of a Form of Godliness That Has No Power

Having a form of godliness, but denying the power thereof: from such turn away. (2 Timothy 3:5)

Beware of Fruitless Learning

Ever learning, and never able to come to the knowledge of the truth. (2 Timothy 3:7)

Beware of Persecution

Yea, and all that will live godly in Christ Jesus shall suffer persecution. (2 Timothy 3:12)

Beware That Things Will Get Worse and Worse

But evil men and seducers shall wax worse and worse, deceiving, and being deceived. (2 Timothy 3:13)

Beware of Those Not Enduring Sound Doctrine

For the time will come when they will not endure sound doctrine; but after their own lusts shall they heap to themselves teachers, having itching ears; And they shall turn away their ears from the truth, and shall be turned unto fables. (2 Timothy 4:3-4)

Beware of Letting What You Have Heard Slip

Therefore we ought to give the more earnest heed to the things which we have heard, lest at any time we should let them slip. (Hebrews 2:1)

Beware of Various and Strange Doctrines

Be not carried about with divers and strange doctrines. (Hebrews 13:9)

Beware of Double–Minded Men

A double minded man is unstable in all his ways. (James 1:8)

Beware of Faith Without Works

Even so faith, if it hath not works, is dead, being alone. (James 2:17)

Beware of Adopting the World's Ways

Ye adulterers and adulteresses, know ye not that the friendship of the world is enmity with God? whosoever therefore will be a friend of the world is the enemy of God. (James 4:4)

Beware of Fiery Trials

Beloved, think it not strange concerning the fiery trial which is to try you, as though some strange thing happened unto you. (1 Peter 4:12)

Beware of the Devil

Be sober, be vigilant; because your adversary the devil, as a roaring lion, walketh about, seeking whom he may devour: Whom resist stedfast in the faith, knowing that the same afflictions are accomplished in your brethren that are in the world. (1 Peter 5:8-9)

Beware of Cunningly Devised Fables

For we have not followed cunningly devised fables, when we made known unto you the power and coming of our Lord Jesus Christ, but were eyewitnesses of his majesty. (2 Peter:1:16)

Beware of the World Hating You

Marvel not, my brethren, if the world hate you. (1 John 3:13)

Beware of Damnable Heresies

But there were false prophets also among the people, even as there shall be false teachers among you, who privily shall bring in damnable heresies, even denying the Lord that bought them, and bring upon themselves swift destruction. (2 Peter 2:1)

Beware of Falling From Your Own Steadfastness

Ye therefore, beloved, seeing ye know these things before, beware lest ye also, being led away with the error of the wicked, fall from your own stedfastness. (2 Peter 3:17)

Beware That There are Many Antichrists

Little children, it is the last time: and as ye have heard that antichrist shall come, even now are there many antichrists; whereby we know that it is the last time. (1 John 2:18)

Beware of Those Who Do Not Continue With You

They went out from us, but they were not of us; for if they had been of us, they would no doubt have continued with us: but they went out, that they might be made manifest that they were not all of us. (1 John 2:19)

Beware of Deceptive Spirits

Beloved, believe not every spirit, but try the spirits whether they are of God: because many false prophets are gone out into the world. (1 John 4:1)

Beware of Those Who Deny Jesus Christ Came in the Flesh

For many deceivers are entered into the world, who confess not that Jesus Christ is come in the flesh. This is a deceiver and an antichrist. (2 John 1:7)

Beware of Those Who Abide Not in the Doctrine of Christ

Whosoever transgresseth, and abideth not in the doctrine of Christ, hath not God. He that abideth in the doctrine of Christ, he hath both the Father and the Son. (2 John 1:9)

Beware of Ungodly Men Who Creep Into the Church

For there are certain men crept in unawares, who were before of old ordained to this condemnation, ungodly men, turning the grace of our God into lasciviousness, and denying the only Lord God, and our Lord Jesus Christ. (Jude 1:4)

Beware of Losing Your First Love

Nevertheless I have somewhat against thee, because thou hast left thy first love. Remember therefore from whence thou art fallen, and repent, and do the first works; or else I will come unto thee quickly, and will remove thy candlestick out of his place, except thou repent. (Revelation 2:4-5)

Beware of Being Lukewarm

I know thy works, that thou art neither cold nor hot: I would thou wert cold or hot. So then because thou art lukewarm, and neither cold nor hot, I will spue thee out of my mouth. (Revelation 3:15-16)

Beware of Antichrist

And I stood upon the sand of the sea, and saw a beast rise up out of the sea, having seven heads and ten horns, and upon his horns ten crowns, and upon his heads the name of blasphemy. (Revelation 13:1)

YET ALWAYS REJOICE

YET AS WE stand watchful with all of these warnings to take heed and beware, we must continue to rejoice—no matter what!

> Although the fig tree shall not blossom, neither shall fruit be in the vines; the labour of the olive shall fail, and the fields shall yield no meat; the flock shall be cut off from the fold, and there shall be no herd in the stalls: Yet I will rejoice in the LORD, I will joy in the God of my salvation. The LORD God is my strength, and he will make my feet like hinds' feet, and he will make me to walk upon mine high places. (Habakkuk 3:17-19)

Now unto him that is able to do exceeding abundantly above all that we ask or think, according to the power that worketh in us. (Ephesians 3:20)

9

Be Encouraged

> But exhort one another daily, while it is called To day; lest any of you be hardened through the deceitfulness of sin. (Hebrews 3:13)

While we are to beware, watch, pray, repent, contend for the faith, fight the good fight, and hold fast as we press on and endure to the end, we must never forget that God is forever for us and forever with us. He never leaves us nor forsakes us; and His love is everlasting. He is our ever present source of spiritual sustenance and support. May we always be encouraged by His love and care:

Encouraged by Thy love and care
I bend suppliant knee
And offer in Thy house of prayer,
My vows, O Lord to Thee.

Benjamin Beddome (1717-1795)

The selected verses on the next page offer some of the hope and encouragement that is given to all who look to Him as the author and finisher of their faith.

Be Encouraged

100 SELECTED VERSES

— OLD TESTAMENT —

The Lord Is Our Strength and Our Song

The LORD is my strength and song, and he is become my salvation: he is my God, and I will prepare him an habitation. (Exodus 15:2)

The Lord Will Fight For Us

For the LORD your God is he that goeth with you, to fight for you against your enemies, to save you. (Deuteronomy 20:4)

The Lord Will Not Fail Us or Forsake Us

Be strong and of a good courage, fear not, nor be afraid of them: for the LORD thy God, he it is that doth go with thee; he will not fail thee, nor forsake thee. (Deuteronomy 31:6)

The Lord Is With Us Wherever We Go

Have not I commanded thee? Be strong and of a good courage; be not afraid, neither be thou dismayed: for the LORD thy God is with thee whithersoever thou goest. (Joshua 1:9)

The Lord Is Our Refuge

The LORD also will be a refuge for the oppressed, a refuge in times of trouble. (Psalm 9:9)

The Lord Will Show Us the Path of Life

Thou wilt show me the path of life: in thy presence is fulness of joy; at thy right hand there are pleasures for evermore. (Psalm 16:11)

God Inhabits Our Praises

But thou art holy, O thou that inhabitest the praises of Israel. (Psalm 22:3)

God Helps Us to be Still and Rest

He maketh me to lie down in green pastures: he leadeth me beside the still waters. (Psalm 23:2)

God Comforts Us Through the Darkness

Yea, though I walk through the valley of the shadow of death, I will fear no evil: for thou art with me; thy rod and thy staff they comfort me. (Psalm 23:4)

The Lord Is Our Light and Salvation

The LORD is my light and my salvation; whom shall I fear? the LORD is the strength of my life; of whom shall I be afraid? (Psalm 27:1)

The Lord Gives Us Strength and Peace

The LORD will give strength unto his people; the LORD will bless his people with peace. (Psalm 29:11)

The Lord Strengthens Our Heart

Be of good courage, and he shall strengthen your heart, all ye that hope in the LORD. (Psalm 31:24)

God Instructs, Teaches, and Guides Us

I will instruct thee and teach thee in the way which thou shalt go: I will guide thee with mine eye. (Psalm 32:8)

The Angel of the Lord Camps Around Us

The angel of the LORD encampeth round about them that fear him, and delivereth them. (Psalm 34:7)

God Delivers Us From Our Afflictions

Many are the afflictions of the righteous: but the LORD delivereth him out of them all. (Psalm 34:19)

The Lord Delivers Us From the Wicked

And the Lord shall help them, and deliver them: he shall deliver them from the wicked, and save them, because they trust in him. (Psalm 37:40)

The Upright Shall Not be Ashamed in the Evil Time

The LORD knoweth the days of the upright: and their inheritance shall be for ever. They shall not be ashamed in the evil time: and in the days of famine they shall be satisfied. (Psalm 37:18-19)

God Is a Very Present Help in Trouble

God is our refuge and strength, a very present help in trouble. Therefore will not we fear, though the earth be removed, and though the mountains be carried into the midst of the sea. (Psalm 46:1-2)

God Is Our God Forever and Ever

For this God is our God for ever and ever: he will be our guide even unto death. (Psalm 48:14)

God Will Deliver Us in the Day of Trouble

And call upon me in the day of trouble: I will deliver thee, and thou shalt glorify me. (Psalm 50:15)

The Lord Will Sustain Us

Cast thy burden upon the LORD, and he shall sustain thee: he shall never suffer the righteous to be moved. (Psalm 55:22)

Through God We Will Do Valiantly

Through God we shall do valiantly: for he it is that shall tread down our enemies. (Psalm 60:12)

God Gives Us Grace and Glory

For the LORD God is a sun and shield: the LORD will give grace and glory: no good thing will he withhold from them that walk uprightly. (Psalm 84:11)

God Answers Us in Times of Trouble

In the day of my trouble I will call upon thee: for thou wilt answer me. (Psalm 86:7)

God Comforts the Many Thoughts Within Us

In the multitude of my thoughts within me thy comforts delight my soul. (Psalm 94:19)

God Satisfies the Longing Soul

For he satisfieth the longing soul, and filleth the hungry soul with goodness. (Psalm 107:9)

God's Word Is a Lamp and a Light on Our Path

Thy word is a lamp unto my feet, and a light unto my path. (Psalm 119:105)

Our Help Comes From the Lord

I will lift up mine eyes unto the hills, from whence cometh my help. My help cometh from the Lord, which made heaven and earth. (Psalm 121:1-2)

The Lord Is Around His People

As the mountains are round about Jerusalem, so the Lord is round about his people from henceforth even for ever. (Psalm 125:2)

God Turns Sorrow Into Joy

They that sow in tears shall reap in joy. (Psalm 126:5)

God Will Perfect Us

The Lord will perfect that which concerneth me. (Psalm 138:8)

The Lord Is Near When Called Upon in Truth

The Lord is nigh unto all them that call upon him, to all that call upon him in truth. (Psalm 145:18)

The Lord Will Direct Our Paths

In all thy ways acknowledge him, and he shall direct thy paths. (Proverbs 3:6)

God Is Our Salvation

Behold, God is my salvation; I will trust, and not be afraid: for the LORD JEHOVAH is my strength and my song; he also is become my salvation. (Isaiah 12:2)

God Is Our Peace

Thou wilt keep him in perfect peace, whose mind is stayed on thee: because he trusteth in thee. (Isaiah 26:3)

God Gives Power to the Faint

He giveth power to the faint; and to them that have no might he increaseth strength. (Isaiah 40:29)

God Renews Our Strength

But they that wait upon the LORD shall renew their strength; they shall mount up with wings as eagles; they shall run, and not be weary; and they shall walk, and not faint. (Isaiah 40:31)

God Will Uphold Us

Fear thou not; for I am with thee: be not dismayed; for I am thy God: I will strengthen thee; yea, I will help thee; yea, I will uphold thee with the right hand of my righteousness. (Isaiah 41:10)

God Is With Us in Our Trials

When thou passest through the waters, I will be with thee; and through the rivers, they shall not overflow thee: when thou walkest through the fire, thou shalt not be burned; neither shall the flame kindle upon thee. (Isaiah 43:2)

God Will Carry Us

And even to your old age I am he; and even to hoar hairs will I carry you: I have made, and I will bear; even I will carry, and will deliver you. (Isaiah 46:4)

God Will Help Us

For the Lord God will help me; therefore shall I not be confounded: therefore have I set my face like a flint, and I know that I shall not be ashamed. (Isaiah 50:7)

God Protects Us

No weapon that is formed against thee shall prosper. (Isaiah 54:17)

God Guides Us Continually

And the Lord shall guide thee continually, and satisfy thy soul in drought, and make fat thy bones: and thou shalt be like a watered garden, and like a spring of water, whose waters fail not. (Isaiah 58:11)

God Lifts Up His Standard Against Our Enemy

When the enemy shall come in like a flood, the Spirit of the Lord shall lift up a standard against him. (Isaiah 59:19)

God Provides Rest For Our Souls

Thus saith the Lord, Stand ye in the ways, and see, and ask for the old paths, where is the good way, and walk therein, and ye shall find rest for your souls. (Jeremiah 6:16)

Nothing Is Too Hard For God

Ah Lord God! behold, thou hast made the heaven and the earth by thy great power and stretched out arm, and there is nothing too hard for thee. (Jeremiah 32:17)

God Will Show Us Great Things

Call unto me, and I will answer thee, and show thee great and mighty things, which thou knowest not. (Jeremiah 33:3)

God's Faithfulness Is Great

It is of the Lord's mercies that we are not consumed, because his compassions fail not. They are new every morning: great is thy faithfulness. (Lamentations 3:22-23)

God Is Our Stronghold

The Lord is good, a strong hold in the day of trouble; and he knoweth them that trust in him. (Nahum 1:7)

God Is Our Strength

The Lord God is my strength, and he will make my feet like hinds' feet, and he will make me to walk upon mine high places. (Habakkuk 3:19)

God Is Mighty and He Is With Us

The Lord thy God in the midst of thee is mighty; he will save, he will rejoice over thee with joy; he will rest in his love, he will joy over thee with singing. (Zephaniah 3:17)

— NEW TESTAMENT VERSES —

Ask and Receive, Seek and Find

Ask, and it shall be given you; seek, and ye shall find; knock, and it shall be opened unto you: For every one that asketh receiveth; and he that seeketh findeth; and to him that knocketh it shall be opened. (Matthew 7:7-8)

The Lord Gives Us Rest

Come unto me, all ye that labour and are heavy laden, and I will give you rest. Take my yoke upon you, and learn of me; for I am meek and lowly in heart: and ye shall find rest unto your souls. For my yoke is easy, and my burden is light. (Matthew 11:28-30)

All Things Are Possible With God

But Jesus beheld them, and said unto them, With men this is impossible; but with God all things are possible. (Matthew 19:26)

The Lord Is With Us Always

[A]nd, lo, I am with you alway, even unto the end of the world. (Matthew 28:20)

Nothing Is Impossible For God

For with God nothing shall be impossible. (Luke 1:37)

God Gives Us Eternal Life

For God so loved the world, that he gave his only begotten Son, that whosoever believeth in him should not perish, but have everlasting life. (John 3:16)

The Truth Makes Us Free

Then said Jesus to those Jews which believed on him, If ye continue in my word, then are ye my disciples indeed; And ye shall know the truth, and the truth shall make you free. (John 8:31-32)

Jesus Christ has Prepared a Place for Us

Let not your heart be troubled: ye believe in God, believe also in me. In my Father's house are many mansions: if it were not so, I would have told you. I go to prepare a place for you. And if I go and prepare a place for you, I will come again, and receive you unto myself; that where I am, there ye may be also. (John 14:1-3)

God's Holy Spirit Is Sent to Believers

And I will pray the Father, and he shall give you another Comforter, that he may abide with you for ever; Even the Spirit of truth; whom the world cannot receive, because it seeth him not, neither knoweth him: but ye know him; for he dwelleth with you, and shall be in you. (John 14:16-17)

Jesus Christ Gives Us His Peace

Peace I leave with you, my peace I give unto you: not as the world giveth, give I unto you. Let not your heart be troubled, neither let it be afraid. (John 14:27)

Jesus Christ Has Overcome the World

These things I have spoken unto you, that in me ye might have peace. In the world ye shall have tribulation: but be of good cheer; I have overcome the world. (John 16:33)

The Holy Spirit Prays for Us

Likewise the Spirit also helpeth our infirmities: for we know not what we should pray for as we ought: but the Spirit itself maketh intercession for us with groanings which cannot be uttered. (Romans 8:26)

God Works All Things for Good for Those Who Love Him

And we know that all things work together for good to them that love God, to them who are the called according to his purpose. (Romans 8:28)

Nothing Can Separate Us From the Love of God

For I am persuaded, that neither death, nor life, nor angels, nor principalities, nor powers, nor things present, nor things to come, Nor height, nor depth, nor any other creature, shall be able to separate us from the love of God, which is in Christ Jesus our Lord. (Romans 8:38-39)

God Saves Us

That if thou shalt confess with thy mouth the Lord Jesus, and shalt believe in thine heart that God hath raised him from the dead, thou shalt be saved. (Romans 10:9)

O the Depths, Riches, and Wisdom of God

O the depth of the riches both of the wisdom and knowledge of God! how unsearchable are his judgments, and his ways past finding out! (Romans 11:33)

God's Word Give Us Learning and Hope

For whatsoever things were written aforetime were written for our learning, that we through patience and comfort of the scriptures might have hope. (Romans 15:4)

What God Has Prepared Is Beyond Understanding

But as it is written, Eye hath not seen, nor ear heard, neither have entered into the heart of man, the things which God hath prepared for them that love him. (1 Corinthians 2:9)

With Any Temptation God Makes a Way of Escape

There hath no temptation taken you but such as is common to man: but God is faithful, who will not suffer you to be tempted above that ye are able; but will with the temptation also make a way to escape, that ye may be able to bear it. (1 Corinthians 10:13)

We Have Victory Through Jesus Christ

But thanks be to God, which giveth us the victory through our Lord Jesus Christ. (1 Corinthians 15:57)

God Comforts Us

Blessed be God, even the Father of our Lord Jesus Christ, the Father of mercies, and the God of all comfort; Who comforteth us in all our tribulation, that we may be able to comfort them which are in any trouble, by the comfort wherewith we ourselves are comforted of God. (2 Corinthians 1:3-4)

The Lord Consoles Us in Our Suffering

For as the sufferings of Christ abound in us, so our consolation also aboundeth by Christ. (2 Corinthians 1:5)

We Always Triumph in Jesus Christ

Now thanks be unto God, which always causeth us to triumph in Christ. (2 Corinthians 2:14)

God Will Raise Us Up

Knowing that he which raised up the Lord Jesus shall raise up us also by Jesus, and shall present us with you. (2 Corinthians 4:14)

Our Inner Man Is Renewed Day by Day

For which cause we faint not; but though our outward man perish, yet the inward man is renewed day by day. (2 Corinthians 4:16)

Our Light Affliction Works Glory

For our light affliction, which is but for a moment, worketh for us a far more exceeding and eternal weight of glory. (2 Corinthians 4:17)

Jesus Christ Is Our Unspeakable Gift

Thanks be unto God for his unspeakable gift. (2 Corinthians 9:15)

God Perfects His Strength in Our Weakness

And he said unto me, My grace is sufficient for thee: for my strength is made perfect in weakness. (2 Corinthians 12:9)

We Are Saved by God's Grace

For by grace are ye saved through faith; and that not of yourselves: it is the gift of God: Not of works, lest any man should boast. (Ephesians 2:8)

God Does More Than We Can Ask or Think

Now unto him that is able to do exceeding abundantly above all that we ask or think, according to the power that worketh in us. (Ephesians 3:20)

God Will Complete His Work in Us

Being confident of this very thing, that he which hath begun a good work in you will perform it until the day of Jesus Christ. (Philippians 1:6)

The Peace of God Keeps Our Hearts

Be careful for nothing; but in every thing by prayer and supplication with thanksgiving let your requests be made known unto God. And the peace of God, which passeth all understanding, shall keep your hearts and minds through Christ Jesus. (Philippians 4:6-7)

We Can Do All Things Through Jesus Christ

I can do all things through Christ which strengtheneth me. (Philippians 4:13)

God Will Meet All Our Needs

But my God shall supply all your need according to his riches in glory by Christ Jesus. (Philippians 4:19)

When Christ Appears We Shall Appear With Him

When Christ, who is our life, shall appear, then shall ye also appear with him in glory. (Colossians 3:4)

Jesus Christ Is Coming Again

For the Lord himself shall descend from heaven with a shout, with the voice of the archangel, and with the trump of God: and the dead in Christ shall rise first: Then we which are alive and remain shall be caught up together with them in the clouds, to meet the Lord in the air: and so shall we ever be with the Lord. Wherefore comfort one another with these words. (1 Thessalonians 4:16-18)

God Has Given Us the Spirit of Power, Love, and a Sound Mind

For God hath not given us the spirit of fear; but of power, and of love, and of a sound mind. (2 Timothy 1:7)

We Are Being Purified as We Look For Jesus Christ

Beloved, now are we the sons of God, and it doth not yet appear what we shall be: but we know that, when he shall appear, we shall be like him; for we shall see him as he is. And every man that hath this hope in him purifieth himself, even as he is pure. (1 John 3:2-3)

The Devil Was Defeated on the Cross of Calvary

Forasmuch then as the children are partakers of flesh and blood, he also himself likewise took part of the same; that through death he might destroy him that had the power of death, that is, the devil. (Hebrews 2:14)

God's Word Is Quick and Powerful

For the word of God is quick, and powerful, and sharper than any twoedged sword, piercing even to the dividing asunder of soul and spirit, and of the joints and marrow, and is a discerner of the thoughts and intents of the heart. (Hebrews 4:12)

The Lord Is the Author of Our Eternal Salvation

And being made perfect, he became the author of eternal salvation unto all them that obey him. (Hebrews 5:9)

Jesus Christ Is the Author and Finisher of Our Faith

Looking unto Jesus the author and finisher of our faith; who for the joy that was set before him endured the cross, despising the shame, and is set down at the right hand of the throne of God. (Hebrews 12:2)

The Lord Will Never Leave Us Nor Forsake Us

Let your conversation be without covetousness; and be content with such things as ye have: for he hath said, I will never leave thee, nor forsake thee. (Hebrews 13:5)

God Gives Us Wisdom

If any of you lack wisdom, let him ask of God, that giveth to all men liberally, and upbraideth not; and it shall be given him. (James 1:5)

The Devil Will Flee From You

Submit yourselves therefore to God. Resist the devil, and he will flee from you. (James 4:7)

God Cares For Us

Casting all your care upon him; for he careth for you. (1 Peter 5:7)

When the Lord Appears We Shall be Like Him

Beloved, now are we the sons of God, and it doth not yet appear what we shall be: but we know that, when he shall appear, we shall be like him; for we shall see him as he is. (1 John 3:2)

God Is Able to Keep Us From Falling

Now unto him that is able to keep you from falling, and to present you faultless before the presence of his glory with exceeding joy. (Jude 1:24)

God Will Wipe Away Our Tears

And God shall wipe away all tears from their eyes; and there shall be no more death, neither sorrow, nor crying, neither shall there be any more pain: for the former things are passed away. (Revelation 21:4)

THE ULTIMATE ENCOURAGEMENT

If God be for us, who can be against us? (Romans 8:31)

10

Walk in Peace

> Blessed are the peacemakers: for they shall be called the children of God. (Matthew 5:9)

God's peace. Peace on Earth. The peace that passeth all understanding. We all yearn for that peace—both now and for all eternity. The Bible makes it clear that God's peace is available to us through a saving relationship with the Prince of Peace—Jesus Christ (Romans 10:9). For He is our peace (Ephesians 2:14)—the one mediator between God and man (1 Timothy 2:5). Yet Scripture warns there is a deceptive false Christ and a false peace coming that will deceive the whole world (Revelation 18:23). By studying God's Word and rightly dividing Scripture (2 Timothy 2:15), we learn how to discern and experience God's peace through it all.

By keeping our minds on Him and not of the world, we can hold onto this peace—no matter what. Many of us learned of this peace from hearing about the Prince of Peace in the Bible's Christmas story we heard as children.

THE CHRISTMAS STORY

And there were in the same country shepherds abiding in the field, keeping watch over their flock by night. And, lo, the angel of the Lord came upon them, and the glory of the Lord shone round about them: and they were sore afraid. And the angel said unto them, Fear not: for, behold, I bring you good tidings of great joy, which shall be to all people. For unto you is born this day in the city of David a Saviour, which is Christ the Lord. And this shall be a sign unto you; Ye shall find the babe wrapped in swaddling clothes, lying in a manger. And suddenly there was with the angel a multitude of the heavenly host praising God, and saying, Glory to God in the highest, and on earth peace, good will toward men. (Luke 2:8-14)

CHRISTMAS CAROLS

AS CHILDREN, WE also heard about God's peace in the Christmas carols we sang at church, at home, or caroling with our friends and neighbors:

Hark! The Herald Angels Sing

Hark! The herald angels sing,
"Glory to the newborn king;
Peace on Earth, and mercy mild,
God and sinners reconciled!"

Silent Night! Holy Night!

Silent night! Holy night!
All is Calm, all is bright,
Round yon Virgin Mother and Child.
Holy Infant so tender and mild,
Sleep in heavenly peace, Sleep in heavenly peace.

HYMNS

GOD'S PEACE WAS mentioned in many of the traditional hymns that were sung in church. For example:

Sweet Peace, the Gift of God's Love

There comes to my heart one sweet strain,
A glad and joyous refrain;
I sing it again and again,
Sweet peace, the gift of God's love.

P. P. Bilhorn (1887)

It Is Well With My Soul

When peace like a river attendeth my way,
When sorrows like sea billows roll,
Whatever my lot, Thou hast taught me to say:
"It is well, it is well with my soul."

Horatio G. Spafford (1873)

Amazing Grace

And when this flesh and heart shall fail,
And mortal life shall cease;
I shall possess within the veil,
A life of joy and peace.

John Newton (1779)

Wonderful Peace

Coming to Jesus, my Saviour, I found
Wonderful Peace, wonderful peace:
Storms in their fury may rage all around,
I have peace, sweet peace.

Haldor Lillenas (1885-1959)

God's Peace in the Bible

25 SELECTED VERSES

God Is the God of Peace

Now the God of peace be with you all. (Romans 15:33)

God Is the Author of Peace

For God is not the author of confusion, but of peace, as in all churches of the saints. (1 Corinthians14:33)

God's Kingdom Is Peace

For the kingdom of God is not meat and drink; but righteousness, and peace, and joy in the Holy Ghost. (Romans 14:17)

God's Peace Is Like a River

For thus saith the Lord, Behold, I will extend peace to her like a river, and the glory of the Gentiles like a flowing stream. (Isaiah 66:12)

God Speaks Peace to His People

I will hear what God the Lord will speak: for he will speak peace unto his people, and to his saints: but let them not turn again to folly. (Psalm 85:8)

God's Peace Is to Be Proclaimed

How beautiful upon the mountains are the feet of him that bringeth good tidings, that publisheth peace; that bringeth good tidings of good, that publisheth salvation; that saith unto Zion, Thy God reigneth! (Isaiah 52:7)

God Blesses His People With Peace

The LORD will give strength unto his people; the LORD will bless his people with peace. (Psalm 29:11)

Jesus Christ Is the Prince of Peace

For unto us a child is born, unto us a son is given: and the government shall be upon his shoulder: and his name shall be called Wonderful, Counsellor, The mighty God, The everlasting Father, The Prince of Peace. (Isaiah 9:6)

God's Peace Preached by Jesus Christ

The word which God sent unto the children of Israel, preaching peace by Jesus Christ: (he is Lord of all). (Acts 10:36)

Jesus Christ Is Our Peace

For he is our peace, who hath made both one, and hath broken down the middle wall of partition between us. (Ephesians 2:14)

We Have Peace With God Through Jesus Christ

Therefore being justified by faith, we have peace with God through our Lord Jesus Christ. (Romans 5:1)

We Have Peace With God in Jesus Christ

These things I have spoken unto you, that in me ye might have peace. In the world ye shall have tribulation: but be of good cheer; I have overcome the world. (John 16:33)

Jesus Christ Died on the Cross to Make Peace

And, having made peace through the blood of his cross, by him to reconcile all things unto himself. (Colossians 1:20)

Jesus Christ Gives Us His Peace

Peace I leave with you, my peace I give unto you: not as the world giveth, give I unto you. Let not your heart be troubled, neither let it be afraid. (John 14:27)

God's Peace Is One of the Fruits of the Spirit

But the fruit of the Spirit is love, joy, peace, longsuffering, gentleness, goodness, faith, Meekness, temperance: against such there is no law. (Galatians 5:22-23)

God's Peace Is a Delight

But the meek shall inherit the earth; and shall delight themselves in the abundance of peace. (Psalm 37:11)

God's Peace Passeth All Understanding

Be careful for nothing; but in every thing by prayer and supplication with thanksgiving let your requests be made known unto God. And the peace of God, which passeth all understanding, shall keep your hearts and minds through Christ Jesus. (Philippians 4:6-7)

God's Peace Is to Rule in Our Hearts

And let the peace of God rule in your hearts, to the which also ye are called in one body; and be ye thankful. (Colossians 3:15)

God's Peace for Those Who Love God's Law

Great peace have they which love thy law: and nothing shall offend them. (Psalm 119:165)

God's Peace for Those Who Observe His Commandments

O that thou hadst hearkened to my commandments! then had thy peace been as a river, and thy righteousness as the waves of the sea. (Isaiah 48:18)

God's Peace Helps Us to Stand

Wherefore take unto you the whole armour of God, that ye may be able to withstand in the evil day, and having done all, to stand. Stand therefore, having your loins girt about with truth, and having on the breastplate of righteousness; And your feet shod with the preparation of the gospel of peace. (Ephesians 6:13-15)

God's Peace Is Abundant

In his days shall the righteous flourish; and abundance of peace so long as the moon endureth. (Psalm 72:7)

God's Peace Shall Be With You

Those things, which ye have both learned, and received, and heard, and seen in me, do: and the God of peace shall be with you. (Philippians 4:9)

God's Peace to Those Whose Minds Are Stayed on Him

Thou wilt keep him in perfect peace, whose mind is stayed on thee: because he trusteth in thee. (Isaiah 26:3)

God's Peace Is Eternal

Of the increase of his government and peace there shall be no end, upon the throne of David, and upon his kingdom, to order it, and to establish it with judgment and with justice from henceforth even for ever. The zeal of the LORD of hosts will perform this. (Isaiah 9:7)

Walk in Peace

Seek Peace

Depart from evil, and do good; seek peace, and pursue it. (Psalm 34:14)

Make Peace

And the fruit of righteousness is sown in peace of them that make peace. (James 3:18)

Love Peace

[T]herefore love the truth and peace. (Zechariah 8:19)

Live in Peace

[L]ive in peace; and the God of love and peace shall be with you. (2 Corinthians 13:11)

If it be possible, as much as lieth in you, live peaceably with all men. (Romans 12:18)

Publish Peace

Behold upon the mountains the feet of him that bringeth good tidings, that publisheth peace! (Nahum 1:15)

Preach Peace

And how shall they preach, except they be sent? as it is written, How beautiful are the feet of them that preach the gospel of peace, and bring glad tidings of good things! (Romans 10:15)

Follow Peace

Follow peace with all men, and holiness, without which no man shall see the Lord. (Hebrews 12:14)

Have Peace

Salt is good: but if the salt have lost his saltness, wherewith will ye season it? Have salt in yourselves, and have peace one with another. (Mark 9:50)

Counsel Peace

Deceit is in the heart of them that imagine evil: but to the counsellors of peace is joy. (Proverbs 12:20)

Be at Peace

And we beseech you, brethren, to know them which labour among you, and are over you in the Lord, and admonish you; And to esteem them very highly in love for their work's sake. And be at peace among yourselves. (1Thessalonians 5:12-13)

Keep Peace

Endeavouring to keep the unity of the Spirit in the bond of peace. (Ephesians 4:3)

Be Found in Peace

Nevertheless we, according to his promise, look for new heavens and a new earth, wherein dwelleth righteousness. Wherefore, beloved, seeing that ye look for such things, be diligent that ye may be found of him in peace, without spot, and blameless. (2 Peter 3:12-14)

PRAYERFUL BLESSING FOR PEACE

CAMPED AT THE foot of Mount Sinai for months, the Israelites were ready to head out again for the promised land. Before leaving, God gave Moses a blessing to be shared with Aaron and his sons that was to be blessed upon the people. God concluded this prayerful blessing by giving His all-encompassing "shalom" peace—a peace that denotes safety, soundness, wholeness, health, prosperity, and welfare upon each and every person.[1]

> The LORD bless thee, and keep thee: The LORD make his face shine upon thee, and be gracious unto thee: The LORD lift up his countenance upon thee, and give thee peace. (Numbers 6:24-26)

May this same blessing rest upon you as you endeavor to extend God's peace to others in this lost and fallen world. And as night comes on, may we continually abide in our Lord and Savior Jesus Christ—through it all.

> Abide in me, and I in you. As the branch cannot bear fruit of itself, except it abide in the vine; no more can ye, except ye abide in me. (John 15:4)

ABIDE WITH ME

Abide with me; fast falls the eventide;
The darkness deepens; Lord, with me abide;
When other helpers fail and comforts flee,
Help of the helpless, oh, abide with me.

Swift to its close ebbs out life's little day;
Earth's joys grow dim, its glories pass away;
Change and decay in all around I see—
O Thou who changest not, abide with me.

I need Thy presence every passing hour;
What but Thy grace can foil the tempter's pow'r?
Who, like Thyself, my guide and stay can be?
Through cloud and sunshine, Lord, abide with me.

I fear no foe, with Thee at hand to bless;
Ills have no weight, and tears no bitterness;
Where is death's sting? Where, grave, thy victory?
I triumph still, if Thou abide with me.

Hold Thou Thy cross before my closing eyes;
Shine through the gloom and point me to the skies;
Heav'n's morning breaks, and Earth's vain shadows flee;
In life, in death, O Lord, abide with me.

Henry F. Lyte (1847)

Endnotes

Chapter 1: The Big Picture

1. Steve and Sarah Berger, *Have Heart: Bridging the Gulf Between Heaven and Earth* (Grace Chapel, August 2010), p. 100.

2. Marilyn Ferguson, *The Aquarian Conspiracy: Personal and Social Transformation in the 1970s* (Los Angeles, CA: J.P. Tarcher, Inc., 1980), p. 27.

3. Warren B. Smith, *Be Still and Know That You are Not God: God is Not "in" Everyone and Everything* (Roseburg, OR: Lighthouse Trails Publishing, 2015).

4. *A Course in Miracles: Combined Volume* (Glen Allen, CA: Foundation for Inner Peace, 1975, 1992), (Text) p. 147.

5. Ibid., (Text) p. 125.

6. Ibid., (Text) p. 52.

7. Ibid., (Text) p. 425.

8. Barbara Marx Hubbard, *The Revelation: A Message of Hope for the New Millennium* (Novato, CA: Nataraj Publishing, 1995), p. 233.

9. *A Course in Miracles*, op. cit., p. 50.

10. Ibid., pp. 377, 584.

11. *Restoring the Shack* television series, Trinity Broadcasting Network (TBN), March 12, 2017, Episode 5.

12. William P. Young, *The Shack: Where Tragedy Confronts Eternity* (Los Angeles, CA: Windblown Media, 2007), p. 112.

13. Sarah Young, *Jesus Calling: Enjoying Peace in His Presence* (Nashville, TN: Thomas Nelson, 2004), p. 199; Warren B. Smith, *False Christ Coming: Does Anybody Care?* (Mountain Stream Press, 2011); Warren B. Smith, *Oneness vs. Separation Heresy Now in the Church* (Roseburg, OR: Lighthouse Trails Publishing, 2018).

14. Katherine Tingley, Editor (*Theosophical Path* magazine, Volume X, No. 2, February 1916), p. 159.

15. Warren B. Smith, *God's Dream: Satan's Ultimate Scheme* (Roseburg, OR: Lighthouse Publishing, 2018).

16. Robert H. Schuller, *Your Church Has Real Possibilities* (Glendale, CA: Regal Books Division, G/L Publications, 1974), pp. 176-179.

17. Sarah Young, *Jesus Calling*, op. cit., p. 199.

18. William P. Young, *The Shack*, op. cit., p. 112.

19. Leonard Sweet, *Quantum Spirituality: A Postmodern Apologetic* (Dayton, OH: Whaleprints for SpiritVenture Ministries, Inc., 1991, 1994), p. 13.

20. Ibid., p. 125.

21. Ibid., p. 106.

22. Leonard Sweet, *SoulTsunami, Sink or Swim in the New Millennium Culture* (Grand Rapids, MI: Zondervan, 1999), p. 34.

23. Barbara Marx Hubbard, *The Revelation*, op. cit., p. 157.

Chapter 2: The New Narrative

1. Sarah Young, *Jesus Calling: Enjoying Peace in His Presence* (Nashville, TN: Thomas Nelson, 2004), p. 260.

2. For example, in George Barna's book *Leaders on Leadership*, the term "change agent" is used over 45 times.

3. Sarah Young, *Jesus Calling*, op. cit., p. 362.

4. Pierre Teilhard de Chardin, *Christianity and Evolution* (New York, NY: Harcourt Brace Jovanivich, Inc., 1971), p. 130.

5. Robert H. Schuller, *If It's Going to Be, It's Up to Me: The Eight Proven Principles of Possibility Thinking* (New York, NY: HarperPaperbacks: A Division of HarperCollins Publishers, 1997), p. 13; Rick Warren, *The Purpose Driven Life: What on Earth Am I Here For?* (Grand Rapids, MI: Zondervan, 2002), p. 27.

6. N. L., "Reincarnation" (*The Theosophical Path*, Volume X, No. 2, February 1916), p. 159.

7. Sarah Young, *Jesus Calling*, op. cit., pp. X-XI.

8. *Messages From Maitreya the Christ: One Hundred Forty Messages* (Los Angeles, CA: Share International Foundation, 1980, Second Edition, Second Printing 2001), p. 108.

9. *Hour of Power*, Robert H. Schuller, Program #1762, "God's Word: Rebuild, Renew, Restore" (November 9, 2003, http://www.hourofpower.org/bookletdetail.cfm?ArticleID=2107), p. 5.

10. *Restoring the Shack* television series (Trinity Broadcasting Network [TBN], episode 5, March 12, 2017). Beaver Dam discourse starts around the 19-minute mark.

11. From https://en.m.wikipedia.org/wiki/Lucifer_(magazine)#/media/File%3ABlavlucifer.jpg.

12. Steve and Sarah Berger, *Have Heart: Bridging the Gulf Between Heaven and Earth* (Franklin, TN: Grace Chapel, Inc., 2010), pp. 99-101.

13. Neale Donald Walsch, *The New Revelations: A Conversation With God* (New York, NY: Atria Books, 2002), p. 282.

14. Ray Yungen, *For Many Shall Come in My Name* (Roseburg, OR: Lighthouse Trails Publishing, 2nd Edition 2007, 8th printing 2022), p.45.

15. https://web.archive.org/web/20040509010451/http://www.eric-butterworth.com/html/eric_bio.html.

16. For documentation on this, see Warren Smith's "Holy Laughter or Strong Delusion?" article online at: https://www.lighthousetrailsresearch.com/blog/?p=16760 (originally published in SCP's Newsletter, Volume 19:2, Fall 1994); also see: Barbara Marx Hubbard, *Teachings From the Inner Christ: for Founders of a New Order of the Future* (A Work in Progress): *A Complement to the Book of Co-Creation* (Greenbrae, CA: Foundation For Conscious Evolution, 1994), p. 79 and Barbara Marx Hubbard, *The Revelation: A Message of Hope for the New Millennium* (Novato, CA: Nataraj Publishing, 1995), p. 243.

17. Leonard Sweet, *Quantum Spirituality, op. cit.*

18. Marianne Williamson, *The Gift of Change: Spiritual Guidance for a Radically New Life* (San Francisco, CA: HarperSanFrancisco, 2004), p. 279.

19. Marianne Williamson, *A Return to Love: Reflections on the Principles of "A Course in Miracles"* (New York, NY: Harper Perennial, 1996), p. 46.

20. Shane Claiborne, *The Irresistible Revolution: Living as an Ordinary Radical* (Grand Rapids, MI: Zondervan, 2006), p. 29.

21. Barbara Marx Hubbard, *The Revelation: A Message of Hope for the New Millennium* (Novato, CA: Nataraj Publishing, 1995), pp. 240, 267.

22. Ibid.

Chapter 3: Holding Fast to Jesus Christ

1. Warren B. Smith, *The Titanic and Today's Church* (Mountain Stream Press, 2020), pp. 179-181.

2. Benjamin Creme, *Maitreya's Mission: Volume Two*, op. cit., p. 11.

3. Wayne S. Peterson, *Extraordinary Times, Extraordinary Beings: Experiences of an American Diplomat With Maitreya and the Masters of Wisdom* (Henderson, NV; Emergence Press, 2001, 2003), pp 100-101.

4. Wayne S. Peterson, interviewed on *Bridging Heaven & Earth,* a weekly talk show broadcast on Cox Communications' public access channel 17 in Santa Barbara, California on November 9, 2001 (http://www.heaventoearth.com/guests.html).

5. Maitreya, *Messages From Maitreya the Christ,* op. cit., p. 6.

6. Ibid., p. 248.

7. Ibid., p. 7.

8. Ibid., p. 238.

9. Benjamin Creme, *The Reappearance of the Christ,* op. cit. p. 30.

10. Ibid., p. 85.

11. Ibid., p. 46.

12. Ibid., p. 135.

13. https://web.archive.org/web/20040509010451/http://www.ericbutterworth.com/html/eric_bio.html.

14. Oprah Winfrey and Marianne Williamson have consistently and unconvincingly denied being New Age.

15. David Spangler, *Reflections on the Christ* (Forres, Scotland: Findhorn Publications, 1978, 2nd edition), p. 107.

Chapter 4: God's Truth

1. Per Telephone conversation with Mike Tooley (*Herald Newspaper*, Truth or Consequences, New Mexico, April 20, 2015).

2. Al Pacino playing Cuban refugee Tony Montana in the American movie *Scarface.*

3. Marilyn Ferguson, *The Aquarian Conspiracy: Personal and Social Transformation in the 1980s* (New York, NY: J.P. Tarcher, Inc. 1980), p. 27.

4. Neale Donald Walsch, *Tomorrow's God: Our Greatest Spiritual Challenge* (New York, NY: Atria Books, 2004), p. 5.

5. Dr. Harry Ironside, "Exposing Error: Is it Worthwhile?" (TBC Extra, April 2008, posted on The Berean Call website: http://www.thebereancall.org/content/tbc-extra-30).

Chapter 10: Walk in Peace

1. Terms taken from *Strong's Concordance.* The Hebrew word for peace in Numbers 6:26 is shalom.

Other Books by Warren B. Smith

The Light That Was Dark: From the New Age to Amazing Grace

False Christ Coming—Does Anybody Care?: What New Age Leaders Really Have in Store for America, the Church, and the World

Deceived on Purpose: The New Age Implications of the Purpose-Driven Church

A "Wonderful" Deception: The Further New Age Implications of the Emerging Purpose Driven Movement

"Another Jesus" Calling: How Sarah Young's False Christ is Deceiving the Church

Pressing On Through It All: Scriptural Encouragement for These Last Days

Watering the Greyhound Garden: Stories From the Streets of San Francisco

The Titanic and Today's Church: A Tale of Two Shipwrecks

Evangullible

E-mail: warren@mountainstreampress.org
Website: www.newagetoamazinggrace.com
YouTube: https://www.youtube.com/warrenbsmith

Warren B. Smith's books can be ordered through most bookstores and major outlets (including Amazon) as well as www.newagetoamazinggrace.com. Digital formats also available. For toll free ordering, call 866-876-3910.

Made in the USA
Monee, IL
20 October 2026

66035305R00125